ANGLICAN
ORDERS

ANGLICAN ORDERS

Essays on the Centenary of
Apostolicae Curae, 1896–1996

Edited, with an Introduction, by
R. WILLIAM FRANKLIN

Foreword by
HUGH MONTEFIORE

Also Published
by ANGLICAN THEOLOGICAL REVIEW
Volume LXXVIII. Number 1. Winter 1996.

MOREHOUSE PUBLISHING

First published in 1996 in the UK by Mowbray, a Cassell imprint.

First American edition published in 1996 by
Morehouse Publishing, P.O. Box 1321, Harrisburg, PA 17105

A catalog record for this book is available from the Library of Congress.

ISBN 0-8192-1669-0

Printed and bound in Great Britain
by Redwood Books Ltd, Trowbridge, Wiltshire

CONTENTS

Foreword

Hugh Montefiore*

On the thirteenth day of September 1896, nearly a century ago, Pope Leo XIII issued his apostolic letter on Anglican orders, known as *Apostolicae curae*. Its conclusion was that "On our own initiative and with certain knowledge, We pronounce and declare that ordinations performed according to the Anglican rite have been and are completely null and void."

This forthright and unequivocal pronouncement, which the Roman Catholic Church has never rescinded or modified, is of such crucial importance to Anglican-Roman Catholic relations that it deserves to be memorialised in print a hundred years later, and to be examined in depth, both on account of the arguments it deployed, and of the consequences that have flowed (and still flow) from it. These are matters of moment for all who yearn and pray for the reconciliation of Anglicans and Roman Catholics in a reunited church. This is the reason that lies behind the publication of this volume in the USA and in Britain during the centenary year of the Bull's original publication. The chapters that follow consist of papers by Anglican and Roman Catholic theologians in 1995 given at a Conference held at General Theological Seminary, New York, under the auspices of ARC-USA, the Anglican-Roman Catholic Dialogue of the United States of America. Some of these papers naturally have an American rather than a British slant, but nonetheless they are all equally applicable to every church of the Anglican Communion. Papers at a conference cannot provide systematic coverage of a whole subject, but they can and do illuminate particular aspects of it. It is the object of this short introductory essay to attempt to look at the subject in the round, and by so doing to show the relevance of each of the chapters that follow.

But first, what were the circumstances that gave rise to the apostolic letter? It was thought that a new era had dawned when Leo XIII followed Pius IX as Supreme Pontiff. He produced encyclicals on scripture which took note of critical scholarship, as well as on social matters which took note of the new conditions brought about by the industrial revolution, and he even addressed a letter "Ad Anglos" which spoke warmly of the characteristics of the English people, especially singling out those labouring for reunion with the Roman Catholic Church. It so happened that in 1890 Charles Lindley Wood, Lord Halifax, a Catholic-minded lay Anglican, met the

---

* Hugh Montefiore is Bishop of Birmingham, retired.

1

learned and devout Roman Catholic priest Abbé Fernand Portal in Madeira. As a result of this meeting, Halifax set before himself a vision of Christian unity, while Portal, previously unaware of the doctrinal and liturgical position of the Anglican Church, decided to devote himself to improving relationships between Rome and Canterbury, focusing on the question of Anglican orders. Portal made contacts both in England and in Rome. He had an audience with the Pope, who said "I am now 85. How thankfully I would sing my *Nunc Dimittis,* if I could do anything, even the least thing, to forward this union." It is hardly surprising therefore that in March 1896, when the Pope set up a commission to study Anglican orders, those hoping for their endorsement were optimistic of the outcome. It must be said, however, that this was regarded by Anglicans as only a first step towards reunion. Most Anglicans held strong feelings against papal claims. Archbishop Benson, invited to send a present to the pope, responded to the writer: "It is the Pope's business to eat dust and ashes, not mine to decorate him. Therefore, my dear Mephibosheth, hold thy peace."

There were equally strong prejudices against Anglicans on the part of Roman Catholics, not least Cardinal Vaughan, the leader of the Roman Catholic Church in Britain, who openly rejected the possibility of Anglican orders being valid, and who later was to describe the Anglican Church as a sect "as hateful as the contradictions of Korah, Dathan and Abiram." (No doubt equal insults were traded by anti-papal Anglicans.) Hearing that the pope was considering writing a letter to the two Anglican archbishops, Vaughan took steps successfully to persuade him to write instead a general letter to the English people. So strongly were Cardinal Vaughan and his chief assistant Gasquet convinced of the invalidity of Anglican orders that they too welcomed the papal commission, certain that Anglican orders would be pronounced invalid. They were proved right, but as Professor Franklin shows in his opening paper, the commission itself was equally divided down the middle. When the pope wrote "On our own initiative we pronounce and declare . . ." he was describing exactly what took place. With his commission equally divided, he had to make up his own mind on the matter. Fr. Tavard in his paper on "The Snares of Tradition" shows that this was really a foregone conclusion, since the whole cast of the pope's mind, as shown in his many writings, was deeply traditional. He regarded all Protestantism as a great evil, so that reunion for him could only mean the readmission of Anglicans into the Roman Catholic Church.

We can see some similarities between the situation then and now. On the one hand there was a pope who seemed to be abreast of modern developments, not least in social affairs, and who yearned for reunion between Christians, but who was at heart a convinced traditionalist. There were some pro-Anglican Roman theologians pressing for the acceptance of Anglican orders but the papal consultants were equally divided on the matter. In the Anglican camp catholic-minded Anglicans were pressing Rome to reconsider its attitudes towards the doctrines and liturgy of Anglicanism which they held were catholic as well as reformed, but there was a strong evangelical wing deeply opposed to Rome, while the two archbishops were naturally cautious. Today too we have a pope who is in some ways radical in his views, especially in social matters, and who yearns for the reunion of Christendom, but who is also a convinced traditionalist. Some Roman theologians are urging him to retain the *status quo,* but others are pressing for a reconsideration of Anglican orders, not least some of those who participated in the ARC-USA conference and whose papers are reproduced in this volume.

One vast change however during the last hundred years has transformed Anglican-Roman Catholic relations. That is the difference made by the ecumenical movement and its wholehearted endorsement by the Second Vatican Council. No longer do Roman Catholics describe Anglicans as a schismatic sect, nor Anglicans speak of Roman Catholics as members of the Italian Mission. Their priests, far from crossing over to the other side of the road when they pass one another in the street, often nowadays make friends. We may still be forced by our convictions to disagree, but the Holy Spirit has breathed into our hearts a spirit of tolerance, mutual love and collaboration, to which the papers which follow bear witness. To this both the visits of successive Archbishops of Canterbury to Rome, and the visit of Pope John Paul II to Canterbury Cathedral in 1982 bear witness, as do the remarkable convergences in the Agreed Statements of the first Anglican-Roman Catholic International Commission (ARCIC-I) and now of ARCIC-II.

Apostolicae curae in 1896 was followed the next year by a response from the two Anglican archbishops, *Saepius officio.* Study of these two important statements has been impeded by the fact that both in the USA and in Britain the Latin text of the latter is no longer in print, while the English version of both are out of print. The inclusion of the two English texts in this volume should therefore be of real benefit. *Saepius officio* receives only passing mention in the papers that follow. In a systematic study of the matter it would require as much extended study as *Apostolicae curae* itself, for it is a weighty and scholarly response. It would not be appropriate to undertake this here, but it should be noted that some of the points made in the essays that follow had already been made by the two archbishops a century ago, both as regards the claim in *Apostolicae curae* that the matter had already been settled by earlier Roman Catholic precedent and also in connection with alleged defects of form and intention in Anglican rites of ordination.

What exactly are these arguments and counterarguments? They need to be spelled out in greater detail than is appropriate in this short Foreword. Professor Franklin (who chaired the ARC-USA Conference) achieves this in his contribution on "The Opening of the Vatican Archives and the ARCIC Process" which follows after this Foreword; and of course the actual texts may be read in full in the English translations included in this volume. Professor Franklin shows that it is not only Anglicans who disagree with the apostolic letter, and he gives us a flavour of the sharp controversy between two doughty opponents: Fr. John Jay Hughes (a convert from Anglicanism who managed to persuade his Roman Catholic bishop to give him only "conditional" ordination) and Dr. Francis Clark, a former Jesuit, who has written weighty works upholding the papal judgement.

Apostolicae curae declared, in accordance with canonical principles, that the verdict against Anglican orders had been settled by earlier precedent, but its arguments adduced must be set beside the counterarguments of the two archbishops in *Saepius officio*. The Anglican response must also be set beside arguments concerning alleged lack of deficiencies of form in Anglican liturgies of ordination. The main objection against Anglican orders, however, consists in an alleged deficiency of intention, namely, that the Anglican rites of ordination reveal an intention to create a priesthood different from the "sacrificing priesthood" of the Roman Catholic Church. In the words of the apostolic letter, the *Book of Common Prayer* betrays a *nativa indoles ac spiritus,* that is to say, a natural character and spirit which is alien to the Roman Catholic doctrine of priesthood. The Anglican archbishops in *Saepius officio* pointed out the strong sacrificial theology contained in the Anglican eucharistic rite in the *Book of Common Prayer,* and Professor Franklin, in his paper points out five ways in which ARC-USA affirmed that the Eucharist is a sacrifice. The Pontifical Council for Christian Unity asked for further study on ARCIC-I's Agreed Statements, among which were included questions concerning eucharistic sacrifice. When ARCIC-II published the result of this further study in 1993, Cardinal Cassidy, President of the Council, appeared satisfied and declared that "no further study seems to be necessary at this stage."

The most weighty argument in favour of the Anglican intention to continue the traditional priesthood of the church, to which many writers in this volume refer, is to be found in the Preface to the 1550, 1552, 1559 and 1662 versions of the Church of England's Ordinal, but which is not even mentioned in *Apostolicae curae*.

It is evident unto all men diligently reading the Holy Scriptures and ancient authors that from the Apostles' times there have been these orders of Ministers in Christ's Church, Bishops, Priests and Deacons . . . And therefore, to the intent that these orders may be continued, and reverently used and esteemed in the Church of England; No man shall be accounted or taken to be a lawful Bishop, Priest or Deacon in the Church of England, or suffered to execute any of the said functions, unless he be called, tried, examined and admitted thereunto, according to the form hereafter following, or hath had formerly Episcopal Consecration or Ordination.

This would seem a most explicit intention not to introduce a new kind of priesthood, but to continue the age-old priesthood within the Church of England.

The Preface begins with a historical statement concerning the traditional threefold ministry of the Church. Such a claim cannot be accepted today at face value without further investigation. Historical statements concerning the Scriptures need to be validated by the tools of higher criticism. Bishop Stephen Sykes in his paper on "An Anglican Theology of Holy Orders" examines in some depth the validity of this claim in the light of contemporary biblical scholarship. Anglican theology in ecumenical dialogue has to look two ways, both towards the Roman Catholic theology of ordained ministry, and also towards the scripturally oriented theologies held in the Lutheran, Reformed and Methodist Churches. He upholds the historical claims in the Preface to the Ordinal, distancing himself both from those who justify the threefold orders of ministry by means of a doctrine of development and also from those who hold that a church which claims one true form of the church is falling into authoritarianism and thereby declining from genuine apostolic witness. He suggests a *via media*, according to which the institutionalisation of the Church involves costs as well as benefits, and these necessitate a careful eye being kept on the potential for the abuse of power.

Generally speaking, *Apostolicae curae,* far from having the effect of making Anglicans welcome higher criticism has, it is claimed, tended to cause them to react against it so far as ordination rites are concerned. In his paper on "The Liturgical Consequences of *Apostolicae Curae* for Anglican Ordination Rites", Professor Paul Bradshaw claims that one result of *Apostolicae curae* has been to emphasise a particular moment of ordination. Pius XII in an Apostolic Constitution in 1947 declared the laying on of hands to be the sole matter of the sacrament, and the invocation of the Holy Spirit for a specific order in the Church to be the sole form of the sacrament. This too seems to have influenced the rite of the united Church of South India and subsequent Anglican rites, with a specific collect now used for each of the three orders. He holds that this emphasis on a particular moment of ordination is really the product of mediaeval sacramental theology. He points out that some ancient sacramentaries omit the invocation of the Holy Spirit altogether and do not even ask that a person be made bishop, priest or deacon, but rather pray that such a person be given the necessary grace for his vocation on the assumption that he has already assumed the ministry to which he has been called in virtue of his election to it. Professor Bradshaw contrasts the Anglican view of consecration in the Eucharist with its view of Holy Orders. Whereas Anglican theology is tending towards understanding consecration as taking place in the Eucharist not at a particular moment but within the whole sequence of the fourfold action, holy orders tend to be regarded as bestowed at a particular moment of the ordination rite.

The Anglican doctrine of the apostolic ministry has also been greatly affected by *Apostolicae curae*. In his paper "Anglican Orders: An Ecumenical Context" Canon Christopher Hill suggests that as a result of the Bull Anglicans have placed disproportionate emphasis on unbroken apostolic succession in episcopal office. This view has dominated so much of its ecumenical dialogue and reunion negotiations, instead of understanding it within the context of the whole People of God, with the apostolic succession regarded as the outward sign of the corporate life of a church which holds the apostolic faith and lives the apostolic life. This undue emphasis, however, seems to have been redressed by the Porvoo agreement between British and Irish Anglicans and the Scandinavian and Baltic Lutheran Churches, with the acceptance of an occasional presbyteral ordination interrupting apostolic succession in episcopal ministry in a church which is strong in apostolic faith and life. He suggests that a church must understand ordination not only in terms of continuity with the past but also in the context of the whole Church called together by the Spirit.

What developments have there been in the Roman Catholic Church in connection with Anglican orders during the last century since *Apostolicae curae?* Fr. Yarnold, in his paper on "A New Context: ARCIC and Afterwards", points to the importance of *The Final Report* of ARCIC in 1982, with its whole series of Agreed Statements, including those on the Ministry and the Eucharist, which the Lambeth Conference has endorsed as consonant with Anglican doctrine. This convergence could enable the whole issue of Anglican orders to be seen in a fresh context, removing the allegation of a defective intention and paving the way for a recognition of Anglican orders by Rome. Another development noticed by Fr. Yarnold concerns the effect of Old Catholic participation in Anglican ordinations, since their orders are regarded by Roman Catholics as valid. There are those who think that this participation could mend the breach in the apostolic succession alleged by *Apostolicae curae*. Fr. Yarnold notes that Old Catholic participation was one of the factors which led to the decision to allow only "conditional" ordination to the Roman Catholic priesthood of Fr. Graham Leonard, the former Anglican Bishop of London; but he also remarks on the strange fact that particular circumstances and individual intention also played a part in this decision, namely Fr. Leonard's "Catholic intention" at his earlier Anglican ordination, and his "profoundly Catholic theology." Fr. Yarnold ends with a timely warning that if there are some indications of a softening of Rome's view towards Anglican orders, there are other changes which may make their recognition by Rome less probable.

One of these of course is the ordination of women to the priesthood in many provinces in the Anglican Communion, and particularly by the Archbishop of Canterbury, regarded by Rome in rather the same light as a Patriarch of the church. The new context in which the question of Anglican orders could be seen in the light of the ARCIC Agreed Statements (endorsed by the Lambeth Conference) might indeed have led to their recognition by Rome without the need to reverse *Apostolicae curae* had it not been for the ordination of women. Sr. Sara Butler, in her paper "The Ordination of Women: A New Obstacle to the Recognition of Anglican Orders" traces the the way in which Anglican ordination of women priests has deeply affected Anglican-Roman Catholic relations, and she contrasts Roman Catholic arguments against such ordinations with Anglican reasoning in their favour. Pope John Paul II has made it clear that in his view Rome can never recognize women priests in the light of the Pope's approval of Cardinal Ratzinger's infallibility claim, and this effectively closes the door to further progress, at any rate for the present. If Anglican male orders are still to be regarded as absolutely null and utterly void, it seems that those of women are to be regarded as even more absolutely null and even more utterly void.

But cannot this verdict on Anglican orders be revised in the light of the new developments which have happened during the last hundred years? If Rome cannot recognise women in Anglican holy orders, does this also mean that men in Anglican orders may not be recognised? As Professor Franklin asks in his introduction to the ARC-USA Conference, "on what theological grounds is this recognition still refused, a hundred years after *Apostolicae curae* was originally published?"

In this Foreword I have been able to give only a bird's eye view of the subject. The issue of Anglican orders is of course not the only question which divides the Anglican Communion from the Roman Catholic Church. There are important matters of faith as well as of order. But some remarkable convergences have been uncovered by the ARCIC process on matters of faith. Is it not time to attempt to find a similar convergence on matters of order, at least about male orders? The chapters that follow spell out the arguments and deserve the reader's detailed scrutiny and attention. No doubt different readers will respond differently to the arguments contained in these contributions. We end this volume by publishing three short comments from people well-qualified to respond. One, Professor Jon Nilson, giving a Roman Catholic comment, asks: "Is it not now time, after nearly a century, to press the Vatican respectfully but insistently to reopen the issue of Anglican orders?"

Introduction
The Opening of the Vatican Archives and the ARCIC Process

R. William Franklin*

One hundred years ago Pope Leo XIII appointed a commission to reexamine the question of the validity of Anglican orders and to report its findings to him. The outcome of this investigation was the promulgation of the apostolic letter *Apostolicae curae* with its judgment that Anglican orders are "absolutely null and utterly void."

Apostolicae curae laid out the doctrinal basis for the Roman Catholic rejection of Anglican ministry of the last one hundred years, and it is the background of the current Roman Catholic practice of admitting Anglicans to Holy Communion only in very limited circumstances.

In eleven of its sections *Apostolicae curae* presents the *theological* defense of the contemporary Vatican policy of the absolute rejection of the validity of Anglican orders. It is based on the argument that the Church of England Ordinal has been defective since the sixteenth century in "intention" and "form." By "defect of intention" Leo XIII meant that by the omissions of any reference to the Eucharist as a sacrifice and to a sacrificing priesthood in the ordination ritual of the 1552 *Book of Common Prayer,* the Church of England intended to introduce a radically new rite into England, one markedly different from those approved by the Roman Catholic Church. By "defect of form" Leo XIII meant that the words of the Anglican ordination prayer, "Receive the Holy Ghost," do not signify definitely the order of the Catholic priesthood with its power to consecrate and offer the body and blood of Christ in the eucharistic sacrifice.

The celebration of the Eucharist had been designated as a sacrifice quite early in church history. For Christianity there is but one sacrifice, that of Christ on the cross at Calvary, but there came to be a growing understanding of a relationship between the cross of Christ and the Eucharist. Theologians came to perceive that God had given the Eucharist to the church as a means through which the sacrificial death of Jesus Christ could be proclaimed and made effective in time.

---

* R. William Franklin is SPRL Professor of History and Mission at the General Theological Seminary in New York City, a Governor of the Anglican Centre in Rome, and a member of ARC-USA.

This sacrificial aspect of the liturgy came to be so emphasized that when the Roman canon of the Mass finally emerged in the sixth century it speaks of almost nothing else. This Christian sacrifice came to be seen as being offered by the leaders of the community on the community's behalf, and in this way the theology of sacrifice prepared the way for calling the leaders of Christian worship priests, as in the Hebrew tradition, and by this terminology distinguishing them from the rest of the people of God. Christ's saving sacrifice on Calvary came to be seen as being made present in the world as a sacramental reality in and through the ministry of bishops and priests. For this reason, as time went on, ideas and images of the Hebrew Bible were increasingly transferred to these Christian "priests."[1]

Apostolicae curae argues that the exclusion of this concept of sacrifice from eucharistic worship in the *Book of Common Prayer* in 1552 definitively signified that the Church of England had departed from Catholic tradition and did not intend to ordain bishops and priests in the way that such ordinations had taken place before the Reformation in the Catholic Church in England. The exclusion of any reference to a sacrificing priesthood in the Ordinal in use in the Church of England from 1552 to 1662 nullified any Anglican intention to do what the Catholic Church does at an ordination. This omission of the sacrificial dimension of the Eucharist gave to the Anglican Ordinal in Pope Leo's phrase, which will appear throughout the essays of this volume, a *nativa indoles ac spiritus*—an innate nature and spirit—which meant that it no longer could be used to ordain deacons, priests, and bishops validly in the Apostolic Succession.

Sixteen sections of *Apostolicae curae* take up historical arguments which are used to support these theological judgments. Here it is asserted that the Holy See has always treated Anglican orders as null and void whenever the question has arisen in practice, and that this policy of non-recognition can be traced back to the period of the Marian restoration in England (1553–1558) and is explicitly stated in two papal letters:

1. Julius III—*Si ullo unquam tempore* (1554)

2. Paul IV—*Praeclara carissimi* (1555)

The two papal letters are interpreted in *Apostolicae curae* to mean that those ordained according to the Anglican Ordinals of 1550 and 1552 must be absolutely reordained to serve as Roman Catholic priests. These two documents are identified as the foundation of the unbroken practice of non-recognition of Anglicanism by the Roman Catholic Church and of the

---

[1]   On the historical evolution of eucharistic sacrifice see Robert Daly, *The Origins of the Christian Doctrine of Sacrifice* (Philadelphia, 1978); David Power, *The Sacrifice We Offer: The Tridentine Dogma and Its Reinterpretation* (New York, 1987); and Joanne M. Pierce, "The Eucharist as Sacrifice: Some Contemporary Roman Catholic Reflections," *Worship*, vol. 69, no. 5 (1995), 394–405.

theological defense of the tradition of non-recognition which *Apostolicae curae* clearly articulates.

The historical precedents of *Apostolicae curae* thus center upon the instructions and actions of Cardinal Reginald Pole, papal legate and Archbishop of Canterbury, 1554–1557 (however, only consecrated in 1556). When Pole arrived in England in 1554 he absolved the whole realm from schism and began the work of reconciling the Church of England to Rome under powers granted to him for this purpose by two Bulls of Julius III; the most important is *Si ullo unquam tempore* of March 1554.

On June 20, 1555, Paul IV, Gianpietro Carraffa, the great reformer and founder of the Theatines, sent Pole a second letter, *Praeclara carissimi,* which was further papal recognition of the Cardinal Legate Pole's entire procedure of reconciliation. But Paul IV, a Neapolitan filled with a burning hatred of all Spaniards, grew to detest English friends of Spain, such as Reginald Pole, and in 1557 Cardinal Pole found his legatine commission revoked and he himself was summoned to Rome to be tried for heresy.

For Leo XIII the letters of Julius III and Paul IV were the solid rock on which a custom had been established and constantly observed for more than three centuries "of treating ordinations according to the Edwardine rite as null and void . . . a custom which is abundantly testified by many instances, even in this city, in which such ordinations have been repeated unconditionally according to the Catholic rite." In *Apostolicae curae* there is thus no real question of how the documents of Julius III and Paul IV were to be interpreted: both make it clear that the absolute reordination of clergy ordained according to the Edwardine rite of 1550 and 1552 goes right back to the beginning of the reign of Queen Mary in 1553.

However, two new factors now invite the Holy See to reopen the question of *Apostolicae curae* after one hundred years, and inquire into the matter of the negative judgments of the papal letter. In 1996 we must ask: Is *Apostolicae curae* any longer applicable?

The first factor which prompts investigation is the opening of the Vatican Archives to 1903 which has brought to light key documents that show that the decisions of Leo XIII were arrived at through a more complex process with more fractured opinion within the Vatican than could previously be proved through documentary evidence. The archives now give us sufficient critical historical information to warrant a reopened investigation.

A second factor is the general agreement, witnessed to by the papers collected in this volume, that after one hundred years the time has come officially to break out of nineteenth-century constraints and set matters within the broader framework which is called by the authors of this volume "the new context." This "new context" has one dimension which has been created by the modern Liturgical Movement: the Roman reform of the ritual of ordination which has narrowed the gap between the Anglican

Ordinal and the Roman Pontifical. But above all "the new context" is defined by the "ARCIC Process," the findings of the first Anglican-Roman Catholic International Commission, accepted by the Lambeth Conference of Anglican bishops in 1988, which reached "substantial agreement" on such formerly divisive issues as the essentials of eucharistic faith concerning the sacramental presence of Christ and the sacrificial dimension of the Eucharist which are at the heart of the condemnation of *Apostolicae curae.*

There are precedents for the withdrawal of papal letters when the circumstances of church history have changed. After Pope Clement XIV in 1773 had abolished the Society of Jesus by a Bull expressed to be forever valid, firm, and effective, Pope Pius VII restored that order in 1814.

In 1296 Pope Boniface VIII issued the Bull *Clericis laicos* which forbade the clergy of any state to pay taxes to their prince without the consent of the pope. The king of France replied by placing a ban on the export of gold and silver from his realm, thus cutting off the flow of money from France to the papal court. Faced with this and other threats, Boniface VIII gave way completely and withdrew the Bull *Clericis laicos.* Currently the Vatican is considering promulgation of an official statement in 1997 that will assert that the language of certain sixteenth-century Roman Catholic condemnations of Lutheranism is no longer applicable in the late twentieth century. Similarly, new developments of our own day have opened the way to a possible modification of the nineteenth-century apostolic letter on Anglican orders.

The Background of Apostolicae Curae

From the sixteenth-century the Church of England had attempted to contain in a positive sense both Catholic and Protestant affirmations about orders and ministry, but more specifically the Oxford Movement in 1833 marked the beginning of a renewed stress on the Catholic character of the Church of England. The leaders of the Oxford Movement argued that the established church was not the *Protestant* Church of England, but the *Catholic* Church *in* England.

One of those leaders, E.B. Pusey, encouraged a marked emphasis upon the sacraments as a key element of the Oxford Movement. Pusey fostered a eucharistic revival founded on an exegesis of patristic texts for Anglicans which documented the early and gradual evolution of an understanding of the Eucharist as a sacrifice based upon a typical analysis of the Hebrew Bible by patristic theologians. Pusey also reminded his contemporaries of historic Anglican writers such as Lancelot Andrewes and Jeremy Taylor who had preserved the idea of the eucharistic sacrifice, and in particular, of a commemorative sacrifice, within the Church of England and the Church of Ireland. Pusey contended that the Church of England had taught the doctrine of the eucharistic sacrifice in terms at least as explicit as those of the Canon of the Roman Mass, a point which would be made again by the Archbishops of Canterbury and York in their response to Leo XIII, *Saepius officio*, of 1897 which is included at the end of this volume. Little by little, Anglicans dared to bring back eucharistic vestments, lighted altar candles, incense, elevation of host and chalice, and the ringing of bells at the Canon of the Mass, not simply as empty ritual, but for a theological purpose: to set the sacrificial dimension of the Eucharist visibly before the eyes of the people. By the late nineteenth century for one group in the Church of England "the Catholic conception of the Church and of the Sacraments had at last come into its own."[2]

For Charles Lindley Wood (1839–1934), Second Viscount Halifax, a disciple of Pusey and lay leader of this group, the next logical step of the Anglican revival was recognition of papal primacy and the *corporate* reunion of the Church of England and the Church of Rome. Halifax was persuaded that a Roman examination of the validity of Anglican orders on the basis of historical fact would promote unity between the two Churches. It was this course of events which brought the issue of Anglican orders before Leo XIII at the end of the last century.

In a new unpublished essay, the Roman Catholic ecumenist and theologian George H. Tavard summarizes the most recent scholarship on the mind of the pope in 1896:

Pope Leo was eagerly concerned about Christian reunion. This was, in part, politically motivated: the reunion of Christians would strengthen the position of bishops in facing the secularizing trends of contemporary society. The pope's understanding of Christian unity was of course pre-ecumenical. The true Church being that over which the bishop of Rome presided as Christ's lieutenant on earth, Leo felt compelled to do everything possible to bring the minds and hearts of separated brethren, Orthodox, Anglican, and Protestant, to seek reconciliation with the Holy See. Leo XIII himself, in *Praeclara gratulationis* (20 June 1894) launched an appeal to reconciliation between all the Oriental Churches and the Church of Rome. In March 1895 he created a special commission "to promote the reconciliation of dissidents with the Church." In his letter of 5 May 1895, *Provida Matris*, he dedi-

---

[2] A.G. Hebert, *Intercommunion* (London: SPCK Press, 1932) vii; key Pusey texts are: *CATENA PATRUM NO. IV. Testimony of Writers of the Later English Church to the Doctrine of the Eucharistic Sacrifice, with an Historical Account of the Changes Made in the Liturgy as to the Expression of that Doctrine* (Number 81 of "The Tracts for the Times") (London, 1837, 1839, 1840); *The Presence of Christ in the Holy Eucharist* (Oxford, 1853, 1859, 1865, 1871); *The Real Presence of the Body and Blood of Our Lord Jesus Christ the Doctrine of the English Church . . . and of the Adoration of Our Lord Jesus Christ Truly Present* (Oxford, 1857, 1869, 1885). I analyze these texts in my *Nineteenth-Century Churches: The History of a New Catholicism in Württemberg, England, and France* (New York and London: Garland Publishing Co., 1987); in my "Pusey and Worship in Industrial Society," *Worship*, vol. 57, no. 5 (1983), 386–412; and in my "Puseyism in the Parishes: Leeds and Wantage Contrasted," *Anglican and Episcopal History*, vol. 62, no. 3 (1993), 362–376.

cated the nine days before the feast of Pentecost to prayer for Christian reunion, a dedication that he was to renew in the encyclical *Divinum illud* (9 May 1897).

In the area of English affairs the letter *Ad Anglos,* or, from its first words, *Amantissimae voluntatis,* that was addressed to the English people, was made public in the London Times of 20 April 1895. As it stood, it expressed the pope's deep appreciation of the English people, called for good will, prayer, and effort toward unity. But it did not even mention either the Church of England or its archbishops. And it ended on a recommendation to pray the rosary, a prayer, the letter reminded its readers, that was endowed with indulgences. This undoubtedly pleased Pope Leo, who between 1883 and 1899 issued no less than thirteen encyclicals on the rosary!

While *Amantissimae voluntatis* was being prepared, Leo XIII decided to take up the other aspect of the Anglican question: the value of Anglican ordinations. It seems that, in spite of the work of the French priest Louis Duchesne and other scholars in favor of Anglican ordinations, he himself was so impressed by the negative arguments that his own conclusion was also negative regarding the validity of the Ordinal. Yet he was willing to reach a compromise on the question of conditional ordination, should the arguments pro Anglican orders prove to be sufficiently persuasive. To this effect he entrusted an *ad hoc* commission with the task of providing a recommendation. On the one hand, since he had appreciated the work of Louis Duchesne, several scholars who were known to favor their validity were named to the commission: Duchesne himself, Pietro Gasparri, and an Italian Jesuit, professor of theology at the Roman College, who had previously been on the faculty at Woodstock College in Maryland, Emilio de Augustinis. On the other hand, as he did not wish to antagonize the English Catholic hierarchy, the pope asked Cardinal Vaughan for some names: Francis Aidan Gasquet, David Fleming, and James Moyes were appointed.

The first meeting of the commission took place on the 24th of March, 1896, under the chairmanship of Cardinal Marcello Mazzella, a former professor of theology at the Roman College. By the second meeting, on 5 April 1896, two members had been added: T.B. Scannell, and a Spanish Capuchin, professor in Rome, who was opposed to the validity of Anglican orders, Calasanzio de Llaveneras. There were altogether twelve meetings, and no conclusion. At the last gathering, on 7 May, the opinions of the members, pro or con, remainded unchanged.

Following the last meeting, the documentation that had been gathered was put in the hands of the Master of the Sacred Palace, a Dominican who is in principle the pope's personal theologian. This was Raffaele Pierrotti. It was his task to compose the text of a resolution that would be submitted to all the cardinals who were members of the Holy Office at a formal session in the presence of the pope. This was done on 16 July 1896. The vote of the cardinals was unanimous against the validity of Anglican orders. Although the pope was not strictly bound by this vote, it was obvious that he would not go against it. There still remained the task of explaining this conclusion in a suitable apostolic letter. This was entrusted to cardinal Mazzella and Raffaele Pierrotti.[3]

---

[3]   George H. Tavard, MS Setting the Historical Scene of *Apostolicae curae,* 11, 13, 18, 19, 20, 21. The most recent book-length treatment of our topic in English is by George Tavard, *A Review of Anglican Orders: The Problem and the Solution* (Collegeville: The Liturgical Press, 1990), with most extensive recent bibliography of the topic contained in the endnotes, 147–161.

The opening of the Secret Archives of the Vatican through the reign of Pope Leo XIII (1903) by Pope John Paul II on December 28, 1978, and the publication of other documents have made available much new information which bears on how the question of Anglican orders was presented to Leo XIII.

The drafts and reports of the papal commissioners had remained unknown until 1978 because they were kept out of circulation with other papers in the Vatican bearing on the question of Anglican orders. Now the preliminary reports of Leo's commission are available to scholars in a recently opened section of the Vatican Archives. Here we find the complete texts of the previously unpublished positive *Vota* of Louis Duchesne and Emilio de Augustinis with negative handwritten comments in English, perhaps expressing the views of the negative papal commissioners. The dossier *"Spoglia Rampolla"* contains the manuscript of a positive evaluation of Anglican orders by Baron Friedrich Von Hügel. We find here also the various drafts of *Apostolicae curae* from the first scheme of a full Italian draft by Cardinal Camillo Mazzella, Prefect of the Papal Palace, through the definitive Latin text. The various drafts contain changes and notations in Leo XIII's hand, so that we can see how the pope shaped the final versions of the document and came to his own conclusions. In addition, there are many letters of Cardinal Mariano Rampolla del Tindaro (1843–1913), the papal Secretary of State, who maintained an extensive correspondence with the Anglican hierarchy throughout the period, with Viscount Halifax, with W.E. Gladstone, the British prime minister, and with the scholars Louis Duchesne, Pietro Gasparri, Emilio de Augustinis, Friedrich Von Hügel, and Dom Luigi Tosti, the Abbot of Monte Cassino, who also had corresponded with Gladstone on the issue.

Cardinal Rampolla emerges here as the Vatican figure who is the leading advocate of reconciliation with the Anglicans. There are also archival reports from the future cardinal, Raphael Merry del Val, an ardent opponent of reconciliation with the Anglicans, building a case against the validity of Anglican orders, as well as letters from the English, Irish, and Scottish Roman Catholic hierarchy urging no recognition of validity in the strongest terms.

Giuseppe Rambaldi, S.J., an emeritus professor at the Gregorian University in Rome, has done the pivotal first research on this material, publishing the original French, Latin, and Italian versions of the *Vota* of the positive commissioners, and providing precise analysis of these documents in Italian articles dispersed around various Roman periodicals. Rambaldi's first book-length treatment of his study of the Vatican Archives appeared in January 1996 as *Ordinazioni anglicane e sacramento del'ordine nella Chiesa,* published by the Gregorian University Press. Rambaldi confirms the report of the existence of two distinct groups among the original eight members of the commission charged by Leo XIII to study Roman practice in regard to Anglican orders which was contained in John Jay Hughes's pioneering investigation of the commission in his *Absolutely Null and Utterly Void* of 1968 and his *Stewards of the Lord* of 1970. The archives confirm that these two volumes of Hughes give to us an accurate account of the background of the commission and "an exact account of the final vote in the commission."[4]

We now know for certain that the two groups of commissioners varied sharply in their comprehension of and acknowledgement of the historical circumstances in which the Ordinal of Edward VI came about in the sixteenth century. There was clearly a differing appreciation of the historical data at hand, and a contrasting understanding of the use and the implications of historical knowledge in the formulation of theological principles. As an example of how the new documents can shape a reevaluation of the applicability of *Apostolicae curae,* here are summarized in English the positions of the positive commissioners taken toward the sixteenth-century papal letters which served as the historical foundation of *Apostolicae curae.*

A.) Abbé Louis Duchesne was a church historian, a professor at the Institut Catholique in Paris, and a theologian with a European reputation. Duchesne came to believe that the practice of regarding Anglican orders as null and void did not derive from "an ecclesiastical sentence" given in full knowledge of all the facts in the case. The letter of Julius III to Cardinal Pole of March 8, 1554—*Si ullo unquam tempore*—did not declare Anglican orders invalid, and it is impossible to prove from this document that the practice of reordination was explicitly recommended to Cardinal Pole.

Duchesne studied the registers of ordination of many English dioceses to look for traces of reordination, and he found no examples of reordination before 1570. Duchesne wrote: "The registers of ordination preserved in diverse dioceses of England have been studied in view of finding any traces of reordination. Not one case has been uncovered." Finally, Duchesne maintained that the decree of absolute reordination arrived at in the precedent of the so-called Gordon case of 1704 was not based on actual precedents of one hundred and fifty years before, but upon "very suspect documents."[5]

---

[4]   Letter of John Jay Hughes October 30, 1995; Hughes's two works, with their extensive review of all literature on our topic through the late 1960s are: *Absolutely Null and Utterly Void* (Washington-Cleveland: Corpus Books, 1968), German translation (Trier: Paulinus-Verlag, 1970); *Stewards of the Lord* (London and Sydney: Sheed and Ward, 1970).

[5]   The new historical material in the Vatican Archives consists primarily of four dossiers:

a. Segreteria di Stato, Anno 1901, Rubrica 66, Fasc. 1,2,3;

b. Epistola ad Principe, 142;

c. Lettere Latine, 1896;

d. Spoglia Rampolla, pacco 3.

B.) Msgr. Pietro Gasparri was a distinguished canonist and also a professor at the Institut Catholique in Paris. Gasparri would later serve as Vatican Secretary of State under Pope Pius XI during the time of the Malines Conversations with the Anglicans. For Gasparri "neither the validity nor the nullity of Anglican ordinations is clearly affirmed by Julius III in his Bull of March 8, 1554." In addition Gasparri concluded that the Bull of Paul IV, *Praeclara carissimi* of 1555, was not intended to be a definitive decision of the question but merely "a practical rule for the time being." Gasparri found that Paul IV recognized the sufficiency of the Edwardine Ordinal for priests and deacons and rejected it only for the episcopate: "deacons and priests ordained according to the [Edwardine] ordinal . . . by an heretical or schismatical bishop who was himself consecrated according to Catholic rites . . . would be validly ordained." Thus for the future cardinal, the material succession of Anglican orders was intact.[6]

C.) Emilio de Augustinis, S.J., was a professor of dogmatic theology and rector of the Gregorian University in Rome. The rector of the Gregorian made the strongest arguments within the commission that the historical documents of the sixteenth century proved the validity of Anglican orders. De Augustinis had previously been charged to prepare and had in fact presented in August 1895 an opinion on this subject to Leo XIII which held that Anglican orders were valid. De Augustinis was convinced that Anglican ordinations were valid by reason of their being effected by a competent minister, with a valid rite, who had the intention of doing what the Church does at an ordination. The Jesuit theologian had come to the conclusion that Cardinal Pole regarded as "illicit but valid" the ordinations conferred under the Anglican rite, and that the Bull of Paul IV did not say explicitly or implicitly that the ordinations conferred with the Edwardine Ordinal were not *"in forma Ecclesiae."* In the interpretation of de Augustinis, the phrase *forma Ecclesiae* in the Bull of Paul IV referred not to the previous Catholic

---

Rambaldi provides the entire French text of Duchesne's positive evaluation of Anglican orders, with a historical introduction which shows how Duchesne was involved by Leo XIII and Cardinal Rampolla in the project in "La memoria di Mg. L. Duchesne sulle Ordinazioni Anglicane ed un suo esame critico contemporaneo," *Gregorianum*, vol. 62, no. 4 (1981), 681–746. More analysis of the Duchesne archival material is contained in G. Rambaldi, "Leone XIII e la memoria di L. Duchesne sulle Ordinazioni Anglicane," *Archivum Historiae Pontificiae*, vol. 19 (1981), 333–345. In addition to the 1996 Gregorian University Press volume, Rambaldi's most recent treatment is "Ordinazioni Anglicane e Ecclesiologia," *Gregorianum*, vol. 74 (1993), 277–307, 461–497. Other new archival material on Duchesne is analyzed in Brigitte Waché, *Monseigneur Louis Duchesne (1843–1922)* (Rome: École Française de Rome, 1992).

[6] Pietro Gasparri, *De la valeur des Ordinations Anglicanes* (Paris, 1895); Gasparri's position is analyzed and contrasted with the negative commissioners in G. Rambaldi, "La bolla 'Apostolicae curae' di Leone XIII sulle Ordinazioni Anglicane-I," *Gregorianum*, vol. 64, no. 4 (1983), 631–667.

Pontifical rite in use in England but to the *forma essentialis* which might still be found in the Anglican rite.[7]

D.) The Rev. T. B. Scannell was an English Roman Catholic parish priest from Sheerness in Kent. He argued that the Bulls of Julius III and Paul IV were not pronouncements on the validity of Anglican orders, but that these documents left Cardinal Pole *in loca* to judge if the Anglican rites preserved "the essential forms of the Church" sufficient to transmit valid ministry. Scannell also based his arguments on a distinction between *forma Ecclesiae*— "the form of the Church"—and *forma Ecclesiae consulta*—"the accustomed form of the Church": that Paul IV had insisted merely on the necessity of Pole finding the irreducible minimum of "the form of the Church" for a valid ordination to take place using the Edwardine Ordinal.

The papal tradition of prudent reserve in not pronouncing on an issue until an agreed consensus had emerged, of proceeding "with true Roman caution," afforded Scannell the best reason to believe that Julius III and Paul IV were not making a definitive negative judgment in their letters on Anglican orders.[8]

Today we are able to study these conclusions of the positive commissioners ourselves:

1. Rome in the sixteenth century did not state categorically and explicitly that all orders conferred with the Anglican Ordinal of 1552 were null and void; and Anglican orders were not consistently rejected by the Holy See during the Marian Restoration in England of 1553 to 1558.

2. The vague nature of the instructions sent to Reginald Pole, the Roman Catholic legate in England during the period, suggests that reordination was not the only means of reconciliation of ministries in the sixteenth century. This conclusion is amplified by the fact that Pole himself was not a priest until March 1556.

The 1897 *Responsio* of the Anglican archbishops to Leo XIII, published at the end of this present volume, sums up well questions the contemporary historian must still ask of *Apostolicae curae* today:

Although the Pope writes at some length, we believe that he is really as uncertain as ourselves. . . . He quotes and argues from an imperfect copy of the letter of

---

[7]   Rambaldi provides the entire Italian text of de Augustinis's positive evaluation of Anglican orders with a historical introduction in "Il Voto del Padre Emilio de Augustinis sulle Ordinazioni Anglicane," *Archivum Historicum Societatis Jesu*, vol. 50 (1981) 48–75. More on de Augustinis's position in relation to the Constitution *Sacramentum Ordinis* of Pius XII and the 1985 letter of Cardinal Willebrands can be found in Rambaldi, "La sostanza del Sacramento dell'Ordine e la validità delle Ordinazioni Anglicane secondo E. de Augustinis," *Gregorianum*, vol. 70, no. 1 (1989), 47–91.

[8]   The substance of Scannell's position can be found in three letters to *The Tablet*: 24 August, 1895, 19 October, 1895, and 9 November, 1895. The archival material is analyzed in Rambaldi, "La bolla 'Apostolicae curae' di Leone XIII sulle Ordinazioni Anglicane-II, "*Gregorianum*, vol. 66, vol. 1 (1985), 53–88.

Paul IV *Praeclara carissimi.* [The crucial word *concernetia* is omitted in the key citation of Paul IV's letter to Pole in *Apostolicae curae.*]. . . . The principle of [Pole's] work appears to have been to recognize the state of things which he found in existence on his arrival. . . . No definite directions are given with regard to Anglican ordinations, and conclusions favorable to Roman Catholic practice can only be arrived at by aid of theoretical considerations. The complete silence of other documents on this subject gives one the right to conclude that Pole did not reordain all unconditionally and definitely expressed full powers to do so were not given him.

The opening of the Vatican Archives now confirms that one-half of the papal commissioners in 1896 were "as uncertain" of the historical foundations claimed in *Apostolicae curae* as were the Anglican archbishops. Public knowledge of this uncertainty in 1996 should lead to a reconsideration of the nineteenth-century judgment which was defended on the basis of these historical claims. This is not only a private conclusion, it is the unanimous conclusion of the official representatives of the two Churches in the Anglican-Roman Catholic Consultation in the United States in their agreed statement on Anglican orders of 1990: ". . . we do have much more information about the background of the papal decision of 1896. This has made enough historical facts available to us to justify new investigation and appraisal."[9]

The ARCIC Process

Why did Leo XIII reject the historical arguments of four members of his commission? The unpublished manuscripts of the Vatican inform us that Pope Leo apparently decided that the issue of reconciliation with the Church of England was not a matter of historical continuity alone. To the Pope validity was a matter of sacramentology. The archival documents suggest this interpretation of *Apostolicae curae:* Greater weight must be given to theological unity between Rome and Canterbury than to a proof of historical continuity.

Leo XIII thus decided that historical proof of a continuation of sacramental validity within the Church of England was not the central question between Anglicanism and Roman Catholicism. History is not the question. Theology is the question. For there to be sacramental validity within the Church of England from the perspective of Rome, Anglicans and Roman Catholics must be in one institutional community of faith, which implies

---

[9]   R. William Franklin and George H. Tavard, "Commentary on ARC-USA Statement on Anglican Orders," *Journal of Ecumenical Studies,* vol. 27, no. 2 (1990) 270. Rambaldi reconstructs the stages of Leo XIII's thinking from the response of the positive commissioners through the various drafts and schema of *Apostolicae curae* found in the Vatican Archives in two articles: "A proposito della bolla 'Apostolicae curae' di Leone XIII," *Gregorianum,* vol. 61, no. 4 (1980), 677–743; and "Relazione e voto del Raffaele Pierotti, Maestro del S. Palazzo sulle Ordinazioni Anglicane," *Archivum Historiae Pontificae,* vol. 20 (1982), 337–388.

substantial agreement about the theology of sacraments and ministry, hence the increasing focus on the key theological issue of the sacrificial dimension of the Eucharist as the various drafts of *Apostolicae curae* evolved.

From this standpoint, Leo XIII was not saying "no" to Anglicanism. Today we can read letters in the Vatican archives in which the pope and his Secretary of State, Cardinal Rampolla, wished to encourage further contacts and discussions with Anglicans after the promulgation of *Apostolicae curae*. They urge Anglicans and Roman Catholics to move toward unity in faith before the issue of sacramental validity can be solved. In the light of new historical documents, *Apostolicae curae* did not end a process of dialogue. It began a process of dialogue. The Vatican response was theological, not political. It set out clear theological conditions for validity. Could this not imply, given theological development, that there could be some *future* discernment of substantial agreement between Anglicans and Roman Catholics on sacraments and ministry which could sustain a positive judgment of *future* Anglican ordinations in the mind of Rome?[10]

After 1896 Cardinal Rampolla supported informal visits, meetings, correspondence, and prayer in order to "maintain good relations with the Anglicans" and to encourage Anglicans to continue to persevere in "positive sympathies toward the Roman Church."[11] In a similar manner, the chief Anglican protagonist of 1896, Viscount Halifax, also believed that dialogue would continue. Halifax wrote: "We have failed for the moment . . . but God means to do the work himself . . . the matter is as certain as it ever was."[12]

The unpublished essay of George Tavard contains a passage which supports this more positive interpretation of the dossier of letters in the Vatican archives:

> In spite of the negative conclusion reached by the Holy Office and by himself as to the value of Anglican ordinations, Leo XIII remained eager to promote Christian unity and to work toward Christian reunion wherever possible. This was made clear in a major encyclical that was dated 20 June 1896: *Satis cognitum*. The date is

---

[10] Documents on the Vatican initiative toward Anglicanism in the 1890's and the complex understanding of reconciliation within the Curia are discussed by Rambaldi in two articles, "Un documento inedito sull'origine della Lettera di Leone XIII 'Ad Anglos'," *Archivum Historiae Pontificiae*, vol. 24 (1986), 405–414; and "Verso l'incontro tra Cattolici e Anglicani negli anni 1894–1896," *Archivum Historiae Pontificiae*, vol. 25 (1987), 365–410.

[11] The encouraging letters of Cardinal Rampolla quoted here are to Cardinal Domenico Ferrata, Pro-Nuncio in Paris, 24 September, 1896 (#33180 in Vatican Archives) and to Abbot Luigi Tosti of Monte Cassino, 9 October, 1896 (#33468 in Vatican Archives). Other letters encouraging dialogue and contact were sent by Cardinal Rampolla to Lord Halifax on 15 March, 1897 (#36409) and to Frederick Temple, Archbishop of Canterbury, on 21 June, 1897 (#38245).

[12] Roger Greenacre, *Lord Halifax* (London, 1983) 17. On contacts which form part of the immediate trajectory after 1896 see Régis Ladous, *L'Abbé Portal et la Campagne Anglo-Romaine, 1890–1912* (Lyon, 1973); and John A. Dick, *The Malines Conversations Revisited* (Louvain, 1990).

noteworthy: It falls between the disbanding of the commission on Anglican orders (7 May) and the publication of the apostolic letter *Apostolicae curae* (13 September).

Satis cognitum explains Leo XIII's conception of the Church and of its unity. The Church is the mystical body of Christ. Its unity is a gift. But it also needs to be founded on "agreement and union of minds." And it is for this reason that the Apostles chose successors, the bishops, whose magisterium is "living, authoritative, and permanent," centered on the bishop of Rome as successor of Peter. The bishops therefore are bound, individually and collectively, "to obey the authority of the Roman Pontiff."

The encyclical on unity does not refer explicitly to other than the Roman Catholic bishops. The unity in question is that of the Roman Church as identified with the Catholic or universal Church of Christ. But the implication was clear: All true bishops must be, or, in the special case of separated Churches that would have an episcopal structure, must seek to be in communion with the bishop of Rome. The future readers of *Apostolicae curae*, had they thought of it in July 1896, could have read another implication of the text: Thomas Cranmer had no authority to abandon the traditional Pontifical for an Ordinal of his own making.[13]

However, in the period of liturgical revision following the Second World War, reforms of Pius XII and Paul VI narrowed the gap between the Anglican Ordinal which had descended from Thomas Cranmer and the Roman Pontifical which these two recent popes had both inherited from Leo XIII. Pius XII in the apostolic constitution *Sacramentum ordinis* of 1947 explicitly excluded the "porrection" of the instruments from the "matter" of ordination. The matter of the sacrament in the Roman Pontifical in 1947 became simply the laying on of hands, as in the *Book of Common Prayer* of 1552.

Through a series of *motu proprio* documents, Pope Paul VI reformed the sacrament of orders further. In *Pontificalis Romani recognitio* of 1968 the Latin rite for the ordination of bishops was made to conform more closely to the oriental rite; in the ordination of priests Paul VI "brought closer unity to the rite," doing away completely with the porrection of the instruments. The chief thrust of this reform was to simplify and clarify the Roman ritual of ordination. Paul VI himself formulated the principle behind his actions: to keep close to the patristic rites and to those of the Oriental Church, but by these liturgical shifts he was helping to shape a new context for the evaluation of Anglican orders.[14]

---

[13]   Tavard, MS Setting the Scene, 21–22. This does not mean that doubt is being cast on the intention of Leo XIII in 1896 "to settle definitively the grave question about Anglican ordination," as he later wrote to the Archbishop of Paris (*Acta Sanctae Sedis*, 29, 1896–1897, p. 664). But the archival documents suggest that this decision on the precise technical point of Anglican orders was not meant to end contact between the two Communions.

[14]   These texts in English translation can be found in *The Rites of the Catholic Church as Revised by Decree of the Second Vatican Ecumenical Council and Published by Authority of Pope Paul VI*, vol. 2 (New York, 1980).

Vatican Council II of the Roman Catholic Church marked a point of no return in this line of trajectory from 1896 toward a possible reevaluation. Several of the Council fathers called for a reexamination of the judgment of Leo XIII. The promulgation of the Council's Decree on Ecumenism, *Unitatis Redintegratio,* which recognized, but did not define, the "special place" of Anglicanism among the Churches of the West, opened the way to the establishment of a dialogue between the Roman Catholic Church and the Anglican Communion which could now officially take up the theological issues outlined by Leo XIII in 1896. The first Anglican-Roman Catholic International Commission—ARCIC—ended its work in 1981 with the publication of its *The Final Report,* a document containing agreed statements on eucharistic doctrine, on ministry and ordination, and on authority in the Church. *The Final Report,* a result of twelve years of study, research, and dialogue, is a treatise of one-hundred pages in which eighteen scholars drawn from the Anglican Communion and the Roman Catholic Church express their unanimous agreement on formerly divisive issues.

ARCIC-I's "substantial agreement" on eucharistic theology recorded in *The Final Report,* including specific agreement on the sacrificial dimension of the Eucharist, now placed the issue of Anglican orders in a new theological light, opening the way for joint discussion of the recognition of ministries and the full communion of the two Churches. The historical significance of the ARCIC process which led to *The Final Report* is that in the 1980s theological convergence had been reached by official representatives of the two Churches on the specific issues which Leo XIII had said divided the Churches: the essentials of eucharistic faith with regard to the sacramental presence of Christ and the sacrificial dimension of the Eucharist, and the nature and purpose of priesthood, ordination, and Apostolic Succession.

In its "Windsor Statement on Eucharistic Doctrine" of 1971, ARCIC claimed to have reached "substantial agreement" on the sacrificial dimension of the Eucharist with these words:

In the exposition of the Christian doctrine of redemption the word *sacrifice* has been used in two intimately associated ways. In the New Testament, sacrificial language refers primarily to the historical events of Christ's saving work for us. The tradition of the Church, as evidenced for example in its liturgies, used similar language to designate in the eucharistic celebration the *anamnesis* of this historical event. Therefore it is possible to say at the same time that there is only one unrepeatable sacrifice in the sacramental sense, provided that it is clear that this is not a repetition of the historical sacrifice.

There is therefore one historical, unrepeatable sacrifice, offered once for all by Christ and accepted once for all by the Father. In the celebration of the memorial, Christ in the Holy Spirit unites his people with himself in a sacramental way so that the Church enters into the movement of his self-offering. In consequence, even though the Church is active in this celebration, this adds nothing to the efficacy of

Christ's sacrifice upon the cross, because the action is itself the fruit of this sacrifice.[15]

In its "Canterbury Statement on Ministry and Ordination" of 1973 ARCIC claimed to have reached "substantial agreement" on the sacrificial dimension of the priesthood with these words:

The priestly sacrifice of Jesus was unique as is also his continuing High Priesthood. Despite the fact that in the New Testament ministers are never called "priests" (*hieris*), Christians came to see the priestly role of Christ reflected in these ministers and used priestly terms in describing them. Because the eucharist is the memorial of the sacrifice of Christ, the action of the presiding minister in reciting again the words of Christ at the last supper and distributing to the assembly the holy gifts is seen to stand in a sacramental relation to what Christ himself did in offering his own sacrifice. So our two traditions commonly use priestly terms in speaking about the ordained ministry.[16]

The Canterbury Statement then concludes with these historic words: "We are fully aware of the issues raised by the judgement of the Roman Catholic Church on Anglican Orders. The development of the thinking in our two communions regarding the nature of the Church and of the ordained ministry, as represented in our Statement, has, we consider, put these issues in a new context."[17] The nature of this new context was explored in a letter addressed by Cardinal Willebrands, president of the Pontifical Council for Christian Unity, to the co-chairs of ARCIC-II in July 1985. The cardinal summed up *Apostolicae curae:* Leo XIII's decision rested on the belief that the Anglican Ordinal betrays a *nativa indoles ac spiritus,* a "natural character and spirit," that was judged unacceptable by the pope. This *nativa indoles* was found in "the deliberate omission of all references to some of the principal axes of Catholic teaching concerning the relationship of the Eucharist to the sacrifice of Christ, and to the consequences of this for an understanding of the nature of Christian priesthood."[18]

Cardinal Willebrands uses the phrase "new context" twice in his 1985 letter. He defines the "new context" first by the "remarkable process of liturgical renewal in both our Communions." By this he means the promulgation of new rites of ordination in the *Pontificale Romanum* of Paul VI and the fact that "in the Anglican Communion many member-Churches have introduced new Ordinals." "In all this," the cardinal writes, "we see reflected something of the theological developments in both Communions

[15] *The Final Report* (London, 1982) 20.
[16] *Ibid.,* 35.
[17] *Ibid.,* 38.
[18] Letter of Johannes Cardinal Willebrands to the ARCIC co-chairs, July 13, 1985 (#3470/85/a) 2. The letter can be found in *Origins* (1987), 662–663.

since the time of *Apostolicae curae.*" To the cardinal, these theological developments have allowed ARCIC-I to affirm that "in its judgement, the consensus it has achieved put the issue of the Roman Catholic Church's judgment on Anglican Ordinations into a new context."[19]

In the light of this liturgical renewal, the cardinal drew the conclusion that the doctrinal agreements of ARCIC-I, once endorsed by the proper authorities of the Anglican Communion in a solemn "profession of faith," could remove what Leo XIII perceived as the Anglican *nativa indoles.* This in turn could "lead to a new evaluation of the sufficiency of these Anglican rites as far as concerns future ordinations."[20]

One of the conditions of Cardinal Willebrands has now been met by the Anglicans at the 1988 Lambeth Conference, which officially recognized the agreed statements of ARCIC on *Eucharistic Doctrine, Ministry and Ordination* and their *Elucidations,* as "constant in substance with the faith of Anglicans." In preparing for Lambeth 1988, the Provinces of the Anglican Communion also gave a clear "yes" to Lambeth on both the statement on eucharistic doctrine and the statement on ministry of ARCIC-I. No Province rejected the statement in *The Final Report* that "the Eucharist is a sacrifice in the sacramental sense," and many were extremely positive that *The Final Report* is "a helpful clarification" that "sufficiently expresses Anglican understanding." In the light of the debate since *Apostolicae curae,* the Lambeth Conference resolutions on ARCIC-I assume historic proportions. And further, not only the Lambeth Conference, but now also twenty-five of the twenty-seven Provinces of the Anglican Communion have accepted the eucharistic doctrine and ministry sections of *The Final Report.* In studying this tally of reception, the members of the Anglican-Roman Catholic Consultation in the United States came to this unanimous conclusion: "One may ask if the prevailing mind of the Anglican Communion is still as contrary to the Roman Catholic understanding of Eucharist, priesthood, and ordination as Pope Leo XIII believed it was."[21]

However, in its *Response to the Final Report* of 1991, the Vatican, while approving the main thrust of the statement on eucharistic doctrine, asked for clarifications concerning the following points:

1. the essential link of the eucharistic memorial with the sacrifice of Calvary;

---

[19]   Willebrands letter, 3.

[20]   *Ibid.,* 4.

[21]   Franklin and Tavard, "Commentary on ARC/USA Statement," 285. The full texts of the Lambeth resolutions may be found in the *Ecumenical Bulletin* (November-December, 1988) 19–21; see also for reception of *The Final Report* in the Anglican Communion: Emmanuel Sullivan, "The 1988 Lambeth Conference and Ecumenism," *Ecumenical Trends,* vol. 17, no. 10 (1988), 145–148; and Thomas Ryan, "The 1988 Lambeth Conference," *America* (24 September 1988), 162–164.

2. the propitiatory nature of the eucharistic sacrifice which can be applied also to the deceased;

3. certitude that Christ is present sacramentally and substantially;

4. the adoration of Christ in the reserved sacrament.

In the light of this Vatican *Response,* ARCIC-II published in 1993 its *Clarifications of Certain Aspects of the Agreed Statements on Eucharist and Ministry,* and ARC-USA in 1994 published an agreed statement of *Five Affirmations on the Eucharist as Sacrifice.* The United States text on the Eucharist was quickly crystallized as a short affirmation after thorough discussion of the contemporary research among theological and liturgical scholars on Eucharist and sacrifice, of the popular piety and practice of the two Churches, of the responses of the Churches to other ecumenical texts on the Eucharist, and of the eucharistic prayers of the 1979 *Book of Common Prayer* and the 1970 *Missal* of Paul VI.

It was noted that while the liturgical texts of both Churches are very similar in their English versions and that they are grounded in the common scholarship of the Liturgical Movement, many members of both Churches are still unfamiliar with this common basis of one eucharistic faith and liturgical practice. Hence ARC wished its statement to be short, accessible, and easily reproduced. Here are the five affirmations:

1. *We affirm that in the Eucharist the Church, doing what Christ commanded his apostles to do at the Last Supper, makes present the sacrifice of Calvary.*

2. *We affirm that God has given the Eucharist to the Church as a means through which all the atoning work of Christ on the Cross is proclaimed and made present with all its effects in the life of the Church.*

3. *We affirm that Christ in the Eucharist makes himself present sacramentally and truly when under the species of bread and wine these earthly realities are changed into the reality of his body and blood.*

4. *Both our Churches affirm that after the eucharistic celebration the body and blood of Christ may be reserved for the communion of the sick. . . . Episcopalians recognize that many of their own Church members practice the adoration of Christ in the reserved sacrament.*

5. *We affirm that only a validly ordained priest can be the minister who, in the person of Christ, brings into being the sacrament of the Eucharist and offers sacramentally the redemptive sacrifice of Christ which God offers us.*

The *Affirmations* conclude: "the Eucharist as a sacrifice is not an issue that divides our two Churches."[22] This judgement was confirmed by a statement of the Pontifical Council for Christian unity in a letter of Cardinal Cassidy of March 11, 1994 to the Co-Chairmen of ARCIC-II in response to their *Clarifications:* "The agreement reached on Eucharist and Ministry by ARCIC-I is thus greatly strengthened and no further study would seem to be required at this stage."[23]

At this point the following question inevitably arises: one prong of the argument of *Apostolicae curae* maintains that because there was a deficient view of priesthood and Eucharist at the time of the Reformation, the line of Apostolic Succession was decisively broken within the Church of England, and all subsequent Anglican ordinations must therefore be null and void, even if carried out in the "new context" of an adequate, from a Roman Catholic point of view, Anglican theology of Eucharist and priesthood.

The *Responsio* of the Archbishops of Canterbury and York, republished here and specifically on pages 148–149, deals with this argument well. Here the archbishops maintain that if Anglican orders are invalid because the sacramental theology of the 1550 and 1552 Ordinals is not as fully developed as that of the 1662 *Book of Common Prayer*, Roman Catholic orders are equally invalid because primitive Catholic ordination rites do not contain or specifically mention the full sacramental theology of the Council of Trent. ". . .[I]f Hippolytus . . . and Leo and Gelasius and Gregory," the archbishops write, "have some of them said too little in their rites about the priesthood and the high priesthood, and nothing about the power of offering the sacrifice of the Body and Blood of Christ, the Church of Rome herself has an invalid priesthood, and the reformers of the Sacramentaries, no matter what their names, could do nothing to remedy her rites."

The archbishops drew a conclusion that has been heard again today, that in exacting inflated standards of judgment the Holy See in fact lessens the esteem in which its own authority is held: "Thus in overthrowing our orders, he overthrows all his own, and pronounces sentence on his own Church."

The Status Quo After One Hundred Years

Since the United States Anglican-Roman Catholic Consultation has had special responsibility since 1984 from ARCIC to study the historical and theological issues surrounding Anglican orders, and since ARC-USA had

---

[22]   The full text of the statement may be found in R. William Franklin, "ARC-USA: Five Affirmations on the Eucharist as Sacrifice," *Worship*, vol. 69, no. 5 (1995), 389–390. This issue of *Worship* also contains supporting essays which formed the background of the agreed statement.
[23]   Letter of Edward Cardinal Cassidy to the Co-Chairmen of ARCIC-II, March 11, 1994 (#1278/94/e), 1.

reached the unanimous verdict already in 1990 that the judgement of *Apostolicae curae* must be reevaluated, ARC-USA was one of the sponsors of an international Conference on Anglican Orders held at the General Theological Seminary in New York City in April 1995 to review the issues in the light of the most recent scholarship and make concrete recommendations to the authorities of the Churches. Both Lambeth and the Vatican sent official representatives to this New York Conference and five of the Conference papers and two of its "Responses" are included in this present volume.

The opening address was delivered by John Jay Hughes, whose publications have proved to be the "pivotal investigation and critique of [Leo's] commission's work and of Leo's conclusion."[24] Fr. Hughes's address, in the words of one participant at the Conference, "was a moving testimony from a living example of the case in question."[25] Two aspects of Fr. Hughes's testimony are particularly pertinent to a reevaluation of *Apostolicae curae* in 1996. First he summarizes the three arguments of his *Stewards of the Lord* which contain a classic statement from a Roman Catholic scholar of the contemporary inapplicability of *Apostolicae curae:*

> First, it contends that the Reformers' denial of eucharistic sacrifice arose from a practical Mass system, and the explanations of it given by theologians and preachers, which, at least by implication, obscured the unique value of Christ's saving work. Second, the book questions whether defining the church's ordained ministry as "sacrificing priesthood" is authentically Catholic. Third, it shows that the authorities cited to support the alleged defect of intention in the transmission of Anglican orders point in the diametrically opposite direction—if read in context."
>
> The book appeals, finally, to the Preface to the Ordinal. This states unequivocally the framer's intent, by the rites which follow, to convey the same orders of bishop, priest, and deacon which have been in the church "from the apostles' time."[26]

Second, Hughes provides in this address the significant historical details of his own *conditional* ordination to the priesthood in 1968, conditional ordination being one obvious concrete result and future norm if a reevaluation of the judgment of *Apostolicae curae* should proceed in a positive line of development. Does Hughes's account presage the shape of things to come?:

> On January 27, 1968, in the chapel of the modest episcopal palace in Münster I received from Bishop Joseph Höffner (subsequently Cardinal Archbishop of Cologne): tonsure, four minor orders, subdiaconate and, *sub conditione,* diaconate and priesthood. A framed certificate attesting to all this hangs beside me as I write these

---

24 Tavard, *Review of Anglican Orders,* 11.
25 Letter of E.J. Yarnold, November 1, 1995.
26 John Jay Hughes, MS Confessions of a Controversialist, 18–19.

lines. At the end of the private 95-minute ceremony, attended only by a half dozen friends, the bishop addressed me as follows:

"Herr Hughes, we welcome you into the presbyterate of this diocese. We have given you the orders of deacon and priest conditionally; and we leave it to God what has really happened."

Contrary to widespread press speculation at the time, this did not constitute a recognition of Anglican orders. It was a recognition, rather, that the orders I had received were not identical with those declared by Leo XIII in 1896 to be "absolutely null and utterly void." The American Episcopalian bishops from whom I had received the orders of deacon and priest respectively could trace their own orders, through co-consecrators, to Old Catholic prelates recognized by Rome as valid bishops. This is now true of most Anglican bishops in the world. To date the Holy See has declined to take official notice of this new situation.[27]

Dean Stephen Platten, the Archbishop of Canterbury's official representative to the 1995 New York Anglican Orders Conference, commented on the significance of the Old Catholic participation in Anglican consecrations as a further element of the "new context" of which the Hughes case is an example:

In its time *Apostolicae curae* was a crucial document for the Roman Catholic understanding of holy orders and of apostolic succession. Pope Leo's letter encapsulated the papal position of the time. Since then, however, significant shifts in understanding have occurred. First and most significantly ecumenical theologians would now place questions of validity of orders and recognition of ministries within the wider context of our understanding of the apostolicity of churches.

Secondly, even following an earlier and more literal understanding of succession, the participation of Old Catholic bishops in Anglican consecrations during this century has meant that there has been a confluence of traditions through the mutual co-consecrations of Anglican and Old Catholic bishops. These developments, taken alongside our historical appreciation of the process which led to the precise shape of *Apostolicae curae,* offer the Roman Catholic Church an opportunity to place the apostolic letter of Leo against the background of a broader canvas and so to reopen positively the question of Anglican orders.[28]

Portions of the 1995 Hughes address published in *The Tablet* elicited a response from Dr. Francis Clark. The essay of Francis Clark, "Anglican Orders: A Reply to John Jay Hughes," was also published in *The Tablet*. The Clark "Reply" provides a helpful summary of the position taken by those who would defend the status quo of *Apostolicae curae* today: that the apostolic letter remains still applicable to the contemporary circumstances of

---

[27] Portions of the Hughes address have been published in *The Tablet* (20 May 1995), and this passage appears on 632–633.

[28] Stephen Platten, MS The Crisis of Authority: A Contextural Background to the Issue of Authority in Anglican-Roman Catholic Relations, 17. Dean Platten's essay will appear in a later issue of the *ATR*.

the Churches. In the course of his "Reply," Clark discusses his *Eucharistic Sacrifice and the Reformation* (1960, 1967, 1981) and goes on to say:

That 700-page book does indeed present a very exhaustive examination of the theological and historical context which, according to Pope Leo XIII in his Bull, determined the "native character and spirit of the Ordinal." This phrase refers to the original anti-sacerdotal connotation of the Edwardine ordination rite—shared consequently by all later rites officially declared by the Church of England to be of equal status with it, and to be likewise linked with that Church's founding formulary of faith, the Articles of Religion. It is that abiding *"nativa indoles ac spiritus"* of the Anglican rite that makes it, according to the judgement of the teaching authority, permanently unavailing as a sacramental form for conferring the sacerdotal office of the Catholic Church.

In my various writings on the subject I have pointed out that, in Catholic theological perspective, the Anglican ordination form cannot be purged of its original *indoles ac spiritus* by sectional reinterpretation, or by the intervention of validly ordained bishops (Old Catholics or any others) in Anglican ordinations. (The recent benevolent concession by the Holy See of *sub conditione* ordination to Dr. Graham Leonard was not a theological statement; rather, it has been officially declared that the decision was peculiar to that one case, and that it leaves unchanged the authority of *Apostolicae curae* and the Church's canonical discipline which reflects that judgement.)[29] That the original anti-sacerdotal character of the Anglican rite is still judged, in accordance with *Apostolicae curae,* to be the factor essentially differentiating Anglican orders from those of the Roman Catholic Church, is evident not only from the continuing canonical practice of the Church, but also from recent declarations of the Holy See.[30]

Doubtless, the "recent declarations of the Holy See" that Dr. Clark has in mind are Pope John Paul II's words to the extraordinary consistory of cardinals held in Rome on June 13, 1994 in preparation for the great jubilee of the year 2000. In reviewing ecumenical gains and losses as the millennium approaches, the Pope had this to say on *Apostolicae curae:*

On the other hand, an event which recently created a serious obstacle in progress towards unity was doubtless the decision made by the Community of the

---

[29]   The case of the conditional ordination of Dr. Graham Leonard in relation to the issues of *Apostolicae curae* is discussed in a "Background Statement by Cardinal Hume on the Ordination of Dr. Graham Leonard," (26 April, 1994); this is analyzed in Michael Jackson, "The Case of Dr. Leonard," *The Tablet* (30 April, 1994), 541.

[30]   Francis Clark, "Anglican Orders: A Reply to John Jay Hughes," *The Tablet* (3 June, 1995) 698. In addition to the position of Clark, not all recent letters from Rome on Anglican relations have had the positive tone of that of Cardinal Willebrands. A critique of *The Final Report* has come from the prefect of the Congregation of the Doctrine of the Faith, Cardinal Joseph Ratzinger, "Observations on *the Final Report* of ARCIC," *Enchiridion Vaticanum*, vol. 8 (Bologna, 1984). Some recent Roman Catholic publications have defended the continued applicability of the apostolic letter: Christopher Monckton, *Anglican Orders: Null and Void?* (Canterbury, 1987); Brian W. Harrison, "The Vatican and Anglican Order," *Homiletic and Pastoral Review*, vol. 89, no. 1 (1989), 10–19; and James O'Connor in a paper presented to ARC-USA in July 1987, argued that the letter is infallible.

Anglican Church to proceed with the *priestly ordination of women*. It is an action casting further shadows on priestly ordinations in the Anglican community, on which Pope Leo XIII had already pronounced in the Encyclical *Apostolicae curae*.[31]

Conclusion

That the opening of the Vatican Archives and the ARCIC process allow for new approaches to the apostolic letter *Apostolicae curae* and to the canonical disciplines that reflect its conclusions is a question that deserves wide discussion in this anniversary year. The purpose of the essays that follow is to bring before the Churches and the public the last phase of scholarship on this subject. Such service is not to be underestimated. Scholarship—"with malice toward none, but with charity for all"—wrote Philip Schaff the pioneer American ecumenist of a century ago, "will bring the denominations closer together in a humble recognition of their defects and a grateful praise for the good which the same Spirit has wrought in them and through them. . . . The critics will die, but the cause will remain."[32]

Yet after one hundred years, the problem analyzed by these essays is no longer one for scholars or ecumenists. The theological issues raised in 1896 have evolved to a point at which there is ecumenical consensus. The work of the dialogue has been done. "The opening of the Vatican documents," writes Giuseppe Rambaldi, S.J., who has engaged in the most detailed scholarly analysis of the question of this generation, "allows us to read the documents in the meaning in which they were intended and redacted and thus avoid interpretations which might be incorrect or reductive, making understandings more difficult. For me there exists a growing but unique line from *Apostolicae curae* to the letter of Cardinal Willebrands of 15-VII-1985 to the recent agreements on the priesthood."[33]

The problem of *Apostolicae curae* has returned precisely to the point that had been reached by May 7, 1896: it is once again the problem of the teaching authority of the Roman Catholic Church. A great Church that gives a major importance to doctrinal tradition should be able to explain theologically and historically the grounds of its actions and the actions of its chief officers in withholding recognition from the ministers of other Churches. And if it cannot do so, then the time has come to change its mind.

---

[31] John Paul II, "Address to Extraordinary Consistory on Preparations for the Great Jubilee," *L'Osservatore Romano* (English Weekly Edition, 22 June 1994), 6/7.
[32] Philip Schaff, *The Reunion of Christendom*, 35, cited by D. Schaff, *The Life of Philip Schaff* (New York, 1987), 460.
[33] Letter of Giuseppe Rambaldi, November 10, 1995.

Apostolicae Curae and the Snares of Tradition

George H. Tavard*

The apostolic letter *Apostolicae curae* includes no reflection on the notion of tradition.[1] Yet since it refers to past events that it interprets with the intention of reaching conclusions that will be valid and will have consequences for the present, a certain notion of tradition must be at work in it. It is of course not unusual in papal and curial documents to refrain from exposing their theological underpinnings. This is all the more understandable in regard to tradition, as tradition itself is not a theory but a continuous series of actions.

What Tradition Is

Tradition in its broadest sense is the active transmission of certain data that have been previously received. Envisaged as a totality, it is the sum total of the data that are thus transmitted. In the course of the transmission of such data, the tradition is their totality in the making. When the data have been received, it is their totality as now constituted. In the case, however, of a living society, religious or secular, the totality of the tradition is not present as long as new data can still be received. Theologically, one may say that the Christian tradition will be fully constituted at the eschaton. Until this post-historical moment it still lingers in the successive stages of approach to the eschaton. In a more restricted sense, the word being put in the plural, traditions are specific strands in the sum total of the general tradition.[2] In the context of the church the transmitted data fall into two closely related categories that are commonly designated as word and sacraments.

---

* George H. Tavard, A.A., has held most recently the Presidential Chair in Theology at Marquette University. He has been a member of the first Anglican-Roman Catholic International Commission and of ARC-USA.

[1] I have studied the main problems raised by this letter concerning Anglican orders in *A Review of Anglican Orders: The Problem and the Solution* (Collegeville, MN: Liturgical Press, 1990).

[2] One may recognize here an echo of the report of the Faith and Order Conference of Montreal (1963), *Tradition and Traditions,* which distinguished three aspects, namely, the transmission, that which is transmitted, and the focus on certain data that have been transmitted within particular churches. See Joseph A. Burgess, *Montreal (1963): A Case Study,* in Kenneth Hagen, ed., *The Quadrilog: Tradition and the Future of Ecumenism* (Collegeville: Liturgical Press, 1994), pp. 270–286.

It is not out of place to remark that, as an active process, tradition can be seen from two correlative angles. First, the process has an origin, when someone takes the initiative of imparting previously acquired knowledge to others. Second, the process of transmission is not successful unless the knowledge is actually received by someone. That is, the reception of doctrine constitutes an integral moment of its transmission. Without reception there is no tradition. The active participants in the traditionary process are therefore not only, let us say, the apostles who preach and teach what they have seen and heard of the Lord; it is also, and no less, the second-generation disciples who do receive the apostolic teaching.

Every appeal to tradition therefore implies the belief that certain elements or principles have been transmitted, and by the same token the assumption that such a transmission is both possible and legitimate, and that, the data having been received, the transmission has been effective. Over the years proposals for understanding the Christian tradition and its process have done more than provide clarification and justification. They have also constructed theories as to the exact nature, the structure, and the authority of the Christian tradition. Tradition has then been treated as an idea that needs to be explained. Such an explanation may in many cases be useful, even necessary, in order to make the transmission, its mode, and its eventual outcome more understandable, and the value of the transmitted data more obvious. But explanation is by no means universally required for transmission to be effective.

Tradition in Apostolicae curae

That a theory of tradition was at work in *Apostolicae curae* cannot be denied. Passing judgment on ordinations that were performed in the sixteenth century is tantamount to assessing the way in which Christian doctrines were transmitted in a key period of the history of the Church. This touches tradition at two levels. First, the ordination by which a Christian is introduced into the apostolic succession of bishops is, in Catholic theology, the transmission of a sacrament; it is a traditionary process. Second, the effectiveness of this transmission rests on fidelity to a previous tradition regarding the way the sacrament of orders is to be passed on.

Now the assessment of a traditionary moment in the past necessarily makes certain assumptions regarding our knowledge of the time in question. Pope Leo's apostolic letter points to these assumptions when it has recourse to documents that have themselves been received from the past, selected, and then interpreted in view of reaching an appropriate conclusion. This implies a view, that may well remain implicit, of the nature of the Christian tradition. The reasoning by which the conclusion has been drawn becomes in turn a chain in the transmission of doctrine. It shows tradition in the making.[3]

The Documentation

The historical events that are brought up in *Apostolicae curae* are primarily the substitution of the Ordinal for the Pontifical, the reconciling mission of Reginald Pole, the ordination of Matthew Parker to the episcopate on 17 December 1559, and secondarily some minor events of the late seventeenth and early eighteenth centuries: the ordination by an Anglican bishop of an unidentified French Calvinist, with the negative judgment on the value of this ordination that was reached in 1685 but was never promulgated; and the better known but more ambiguous case of John Clement Gordon, that was decided, though with no new inquiry, in 1704. When reviewing the evidence for these events it was necessary to refer to archival documentation going back to the sixteenth, seventeenth, and eighteenth centuries. *Apostolicae curae* refers explicitly, though not always by their title, to the Ordinals of Edward VI (published by itself in 1550, reissued with the *Book of Common Prayer* of 1552) and of Charles II (1662), to the bull *Dudum cum charissima* (8 March 1554) of Julius III, the apostolic briefs *Praeclara carissimi* (20 June 1555), of Paul IV, and *Regimini universalis ecclesiae* (30 October 1555), composed under Paul IV in response to information that had been provided by three bishops who visited Rome on behalf of Queen Mary in February 1555, when Julius III was still reigning.

These texts were read by Leo XIII or his advisers in light of two principles. Firstly, there was a complex sacramental principle, namely that there is a form of each sacrament and that the minister of the sacrament must have an intention in keeping with that of the Church, which is itself expressed in the ritual. The purpose of the apostolic letter was in part to identify the "form" and the "intention" of Anglican ordinations according to the Ordinal. It is to this search for form and intention that the attention of most scholars has turned in subsequent studies of *Apostolicae curae* in particular and of Anglican orders in general. But the sacramental principle is expressed in a theology and, in the present case, in the sacramental theology that was current in Rome in the late nineteenth century. As such it reflects the scholastic approach to sacraments that was being revived in the neoscholastic theology favored by Leo XIII. The pope concluded that the change that was introduced in the ritual of ordination by the English

---

[3] On the theology of tradition, see my volumes, *Holy Writ or Holy Church: The Crisis of the Protestant Reformation* (New York: Harper, 1959); *The Seventeenth-century Tradition: A Study in Recusant Thought* (Leiden: Brill, 1978). On the treatment of tradition in ecumenical dialogues: John Reumann and Joseph A. Fitzmyer, *Scripture as Norm for our Common Faith* (*Journal of Ecumenical Studies*, 30:1, Winter 1993, pp. 81–107); Ken Hagen, ed., *Quadrilog*.

reformers so vitiated the *nativa indoles ac spiritus* of the Ordinal that the rite no longer corresponded to the proper form and no longer expressed the Church's intention. In these conditions the rite no longer seemed to do what the Pontifical had done.

Secondly, there was the canonical principle that such matters should be decided, if at all possible, according to precedent. Indeed, the first pages of the apostolic letter affirm that there already exists a *communis sententia* against the validity of Anglican orders, and that the Archives of the Holy Office contain evidence that this has been confirmed "not a few times" by "the Church's actions and constant discipline." It is precisely in illustration of these allegedly numerous precedents that the cases of the unknown Huguenot and of John Gordon are advanced. The argument from precedent reflects a canonical concern to follow a safe course rather than innovate. Yet it is not merely canonical. It has at least two further theological dimensions. In the first place it fits the attitude of "tutiorism" that was and is widely accepted in Catholic sacramental theology and practice. That is, ministers should do their utmost to ensure the validity of the sacraments they confer. Neglect of this rule at any time introduces, if not a presumption, at least a suspicion of inadequate intention on the minister's part. In the second place, the argument from precedent implies an appeal to tradition, a tradition which, in this case, is said to be established by documents contained in the Archives, yet a tradition that is not directly verifiable since these Archives are not normally open to scholars, still less to the public.

The Context

If my analysis is, up to this point, correct, then it follows that the argumentation of *Apostolicae curae* should be clarified by research into the doctrine of tradition that was generally operative in the decisions and documents of Pope Leo. This doctrine of tradition is inseparable from the political and social context in which Leo XIII saw the urgent tasks of the Church. I have limited my investigation to the encyclicals. As the most solemn statements that were issued by Leo XIII, they express the heart of his thought and they show his method of work.

From *Inscrutabili Dei* (21 April 1878) to *Dum multa* (24 December 1902), Leo XIII issued no less than eighty-five encyclicals, some of them very short.[4] Twelve are pious exhortations to invoke the Virgin Mary during the month of October (1883, '84, '87, and each year from 1891 to '99). Social concerns are prominent in many others, that betray a profound anxiety

---

[4]   The most convenient edition of the encyclicals in English is Claudia Carlen, *The Papal Encyclicals, 1878–1903* (New York: Consortium Books, 1983). For the Latin text I have chiefly used *Sämtliche Rundschreiben Erlassen von Unserem Heiligsten Vater Leo XIII* (Freiburg: Herder, 6 vol., 1881–1904).

regarding the state and orientation of modern society. Most of Leo's encyclicals in fact open on a dire description of the situation and of the evils that are bound to come if the world pursues in its present course. The pope denounces "perverse" and "pernicious" sects, and above all one "that is called by various and nearly barbarous names, Socialists, Communists, or Nihilists" (*Quod apostolici*, 28 December 1878). Along with what he names "the deadly pest of Socialism" Leo stigmatizes Naturalism, Rationalism, Materialism, Liberalism, Atheism. With vehemence he attacks "the Socialists and other seditious mobs" (*Libertas praestantissimum*, 20 June 1888), especially "the Masonic sect," that has been formed, he says, "against all human and divine law" as well as other secret societies (*Humanum genus*, 20 April 1884).

The pope sees all these groups as one, and he does not distinguish among their philosophies or ideologies. They are part of a conspiracy to ruin the Church, the family, and civilized society. This is evident, Pope Leo believes, in the sectarian claim that all humans are "equal by nature" whereas "inequality of rights and of power comes from the very Author of nature." The equality of princes and their subjects destroys the state. The equality of men and women destroys the family, since "the man is the head of the woman . . . wives must be subject to their men". The equality of all believers destroys the Church. The modern sects plan to do away with all hierarchies and they teach the false doctrine that the source of civil authority is the people, whereas it can only be God himself, the source of all authority. They affirm the right of the people to rebellion, a point that is denied by Catholic doctrine because all authority is from God. They even affirm "the liberty to choose one's religion" (*Immortale Dei*, 1 November 1885). In contrast, the Catholic model for society is hierarchic, "so that those who are inferior reach their ends through those who are in the middle, and those who are in the middle through those who are superior" (*Quod apostolici*). Such a hierarchic model clearly derives from the vision of Pseudo-Dionysius. It is far removed from the actual organization of any political system, whether monarchic or democratic.

Leo XIII ascribed the origin of the dangerous modern movements to "the innovators of the sixteenth century," the Reformers. He selected for special mention the teaching that justification is by faith alone, the rejection of episcopal and papal authority, and the advocacy of the right of individual believers to interpret Scripture for themselves. Yet as he summed up the situation the pope unwittingly echoed the words, if not the doctrine, of Martin Luther.[5] Luther believed that there are, under God, two kingdoms, the one ruled through political leaders, the other through Christ and his

---

[5] Both Luther and Leo XIII were of course inspired by St. Augustine's reflection on the "two cities."

representatives in the Church. For Leo also there are two kingdoms: "The one is the kingdom of God on earth, that is, the true Church of Jesus Christ . . . the other is the kingdom of Satan . . ." (*Humanum genus*, 20 April 1884). Where, one may ask, do the kingdoms of this world belong? It is in the logic of Leo XIII that if kings, presidents, and peoples do not wish to be ruled by Satan, they have no other choice than to be ruled by God through the Church.

Pope Leo's Hope for Society

In a refreshingly naive way Leo XIII suggested in 1884 that the way to counter the enterprises of the Masonic sect was to develop the Third Order of St. Francis (*Humanum genus*). By the time of *Rerum novarum* (1891) he had more adequately gauged the depth of the social question. Yet in all his encyclicals the pope maintained that there is only one fundamental and universal remedy to the evils that assail humanity: obedience to the Church. Being "the column and firmament of the truth and the incorrupt teacher of mores" (*Libertas praestantissimum*), the Church speaks for God. Within the Church itself obedience is due to bishops as "rectors and heads of the Church that each has lawfully received to govern" (*Cum multa sint*, 8 December 1882), and above all to the pope, who is "the teacher and prince of the whole Church", the "vicar of Jesus Christ, the president of the universal Church, the teacher of what is to be believed and what is to be done" (*Sapientiae christianae*, 10 January 1890). The apostolic see is "the perennial and incorrupt source of salvation" (*Exeunte jam anno*, Christmas 1888). The Roman Church is "the mother and teacher of all the Churches." Leo XIII could even declare of himself: "We are Almighty God's lieutenant on earth" (*Praeclara gratulationis*, 20 June 1894).

Leo XIII multiplied approaches to the citizens of several European nations, and even to all the people of the whole world. These documents contained warnings against the evils of the time and invitations to nations and people to obey the Church and to follow his own lead.[6] At times he addressed the peoples as such, more often their bishops. Not seldom did he try to influence political life, fearlessly naming what he identified as the forces of evil. Admittedly a change of tone occurred, toward the end of the last full decade of his long tenure, in the pope's language in regard to matters social and political. In 1888 the remark that "the threatening trem-

---

[6]   One may cite, among others: *Licet multa*, addressed to Belgium, 3 August 1881; *Etsi nos*, 15 February 1882, and *Dell'alto dell'apostolico seggio*, 15 October 1890, both of them addressed to Italy, denouncing the Masonic threat; *Pergrata*, to Portugal, 15 February 1882; *Cum multa*, to Spain, 8 December 1882; *Nobilissima Gallorum gens*, to France, 8 February 1884; apostolic letter *Amantissime voluntatis*, to England, April 15 1895; *Jampridem*, to Prussia, 6 January 1886; *Quod multum*, to Hungary, 22 August 1886; *Soepe nos*, to Ireland, 24 June 1888.

ors of proletarians explode everywhere . . . " illustrated an exhortation to lead a holy life (*Exeunte jam anno,* Christmas 1888). But in 1891 *Rerum novarum* analyzed with discernment and empathy the situation of workers in the developing capitalist society.

Likewise, in 1888 the pope intervened in Irish politics in the name of Christian morality as he condemned some of the revolutionary methods used in the Irish struggle for liberation: "Boycotting," the pope affirmed, is not compatible with Catholic ethics, for, he said, this tactic implies a denial of the right of ownership![7] Insofar as boycotts are non-violent forms of protest, Leo's view of both politics and social ethics was, even in pre-Gandhi days, quite obsolete. Nonetheless, in 1892 (*Au milieu des sollicitudes*), Leo urged French Catholics to ally to the republican form of government. The Third French Republic, of course, had its origin in the Revolution of 1789, that the pope had previously described as "less a commotion than a confla-gration of the Gauls, for when God is removed all society is profanated" (*Arcanum divinae sapientiae,* 10 February 1880). Even then, however, Leo XIII was not converted to liberalism or even to democracy. His ideal re-mained a sort of universal theocracy in which the pope would speak for God.

Society and Church Union

There was a parallel between Leo XIII's hope for society and his hope for Christian unity. Leo was concerned about the disintegration of civiliza-tion. The orderly form of government, already threatened, as he thought, by the Reformation, had been effectively destroyed in most of Europe by the French Revolution. It was still being undermined by the Masons and their cohorts. Facing this, Leo XIII multiplied exhortations to Christians to unite. Reunion would be a powerful weapon against the future upheavals that he feared. But his approach to the divisions of Christendom was naturally tainted by his political horizon. It eventually gave shape to what historians of the ecumenical movement call "unionism": the effort to restore Christian unity through the conversion of all "separated Christians" to the ultramon-tane form of Roman Catholicism. His attention to the situation of frag-mented Christendom did not alter Leo's judgment on the Reformation and the Reformers. It did not prepare him to appreciate the liturgical work of Cranmer when, in 1895, he was urged by Lord Halifax and Abbé Portal to assess the value of Anglican ordinations.

---

[7] Leo's concern about property in Ireland was prompted by Charles Parnell's campaign for Home Rule: As part of his tactics, Parnell (1846–1891) urged Irish tenants to pay their English landlords no more than what they considered to be a fair rent. Leo seemed to ignore the fact that the system of land ownership in Ireland perpetuated a feudal type of society that had been abandoned everywhere else in Western Europe, and that had originally been imposed on the Irish by their English oppressors.

The Tradition

Few encyclicals of Leo XIII speak explicitly about tradition in the Church. The verb *tradere* occurs fairly often, more so than the substantive *traditio*. Yet in most instances it refers to the divine revelation, seen as communication between heaven and earth. Such a tradition is a revelation of truths made to us by God; and this communication of "truths divinely transmitted" (*Aeterni Patris*, 4 August 1879) takes place on earth through the one Mediator Jesus Christ as Jesus passes on what he has himself received from the Father (*Cum multa sint*, 8 December 1882).

At its highest level tradition is intratrinitarian: from the Father to the Son. It becomes christocentric when the Word incarnate teaches in human words and examples what he has heard from the Father. At this point tradition is biblical: It is what God does in communicating with the patriarchs and the chosen people. It becomes apostolic and ecclesial when the apostles and their successors in turn pass on to later generations what they have received from Christ through the agency of the Holy Spirit. The model again derives from the Dionysian hierarchies. It is more contemplative than historical.

As a transmission of doctrine that takes place on earth, tradition, however, is also a historical phenomenon. There are human traditions, received from the past, that touch on the civil aspects of life. Some of them may even go back to the origins of humanity[8] and are more or less vaguely remembered by Christians and non-Christians alike. Thus, Leo XIII argues, "the nature of things, the memory of the origins, the conscience of the human race" agree with the Christian doctrine on matrimony (*Arcanum divinae sapientiae*). Along with many other human realities, marriage belongs jointly in the two realms of the civil and the sacred. Each realm is independent. Yet there should be harmony between them, in that, as regards points of common interest, "the power to which human affairs have been transmitted opportunely and properly depends on the power to which heavenly things have been entrusted." Pope Leo stands in the Bellarminian tradition of the indirect supremacy of the spiritual power over the temporal, and spiritual, in this context, really means papal. Human traditions must then be judged by the Church's traditions. For the Church, that is, the Roman Church, is faithful to the true doctrine, "which Christ the Lord and the apostles as interpreters of the heavenly will transmitted, which the Catholic Church has itself religiously kept and has in all ages ordered the faithful to keep." The Catholic teaching on matrimony is faithful, as the Council of Trent put it, to "our holy fathers, to the councils, and to the Church's universal tradition."[9]

---

[8]   This was a central thesis of the traditionalist school.

[9]   The tridentine reference is to the decree of the twenty-fourth session, *Matrimonii perpetuum: . . . sancti patres nostri, concilia et universalis traditio semper docuerunt* (Denziger-Schönmetzer, n. 1800).

This tradition is unalterable, for it is the divine revelation. But God marvelously prepared the human mind for it, for it tallies with humanity's memory of its origins. And one finds approximations of it in the highest human wisdom that was available to the pagans, as was already recognized by "the holy fathers of the Church . . . , the venerable witnesses and guardians of the religious traditions" (*Aeterni Patris*).

Scripture, Tradition, Magisterium

In 1893 the encyclical on Holy Scripture gave Pope Leo the occasion to recognize the eminent place of the Scriptures among the traditions. But he made no distinction between the Scriptures as God-given and the Scriptures as authentically interpreted. God, he said, transmitted them to the Church "in order that they be used, with the Church as the leader and the most certain teacher in reading and explaining his sayings" (*Providentissimus Deus*, 18 November 1893). Scripture and tradition must then go together. "The holy Fathers have the highest authority whenever they unanimously explain some biblical witness regarding the doctrine of faith and behavior, for it is clearly evident from their consensus that the biblical witness has been transmitted from the apostles according to the Catholic faith." It is in harmony with the Fathers' testimony that Scripture is "a most clear source of the Catholic revelation."

In the sixteenth century, however, the Reformers, "having rejected the divine traditions and the Church's magisterium, decreed that Scripture was the only source of revelation." But novelty, Leo XIII insisted, is a mark of falsehood, and continuity a mark of truth. He accordingly affirmed, in the encyclical on the unity of Christians, that the doctrine of Vatican I on the primacy of the pope is "not a new opinion but the old and constant explicit faith of all centuries" (*Satis cognitum*, 29 June 1896). It is imperative that Christian doctrine be "preserved and propagated in integrity and purity." And this is precisely why "Jesus Christ instituted in the Church a living, authentic, and perennial magisterium that he strengthened with his power, instructed through the Spirit of truth, confirmed by miracles," so that "whenever it is declared by the word of this magisterium that this or that is contained in the system of the divinely transmitted doctrine, everyone must believe with certainty that it is true, for if it were at all false it would follow that God himself would be the author of error. . . . "

Leo XIII did not consider defining any doctrine, and he seldom spoke of papal infallibility. When, in *Providentissimus Deus*, he mentioned "the divine and infallible magisterium of the Church," this was to affirm that this magisterium "resides also in the authority of Sacred Scripture." Scripture is an instance of magisterial infallibility. Generally, however, Pope Leo preferred to emphasize the general inerrancy of magisterial decisions, for otherwise God would be responsible for error. The Church speaks for God. "It pertains to the teaching Church, to which God entrusted the keeping and interpretation of his sayings, to decide which are the divinely transmitted doctrines" (*Sapientiae christianae*). The text continues a little further:

It is therefore not sufficient to assent sincerely and firmly to the doctrines that are expounded by the Church as divinely revealed, if they have not been defined by a solemn judgment, at least by the universal ordinary magisterium. . . . But one must in addition place among the duties of Christians to let themselves be ruled and governed by the authority and guidance of the bishops and first of all of the Apostolic See.

The understanding of tradition that was operative in Leo XIII's encyclicals thus confirms his general teaching that by God's eternal design the Church has supreme authority over all the earth. The Church that the pope had in mind was of course the Roman Church, whose divine authority, Leo believed, resided primarily in himself as bishop of Rome.

The Traditionalist School

The position of Leo XIII ought to be seen in the context of the theologies of tradition that were held by Catholic theologians in the nineteenth century.

According to the traditionalist school, a divine revelation lay at the origin of all knowledge, including the knowledge of language and the ability to speak. This primitive revelation, made to our first parents at the very beginning of humanity, still serves as the basis for the rational capacity to know God and to prove the doctrines of Christianity. Tradition and the right use of reason were at the heart of Louis de Bonald's political theory in his seminal book, *Théorie du pouvoir politique et religieux* (1796). They were said to be in harmony, for tradition is basically identical with the fidelity of reason to its own fundamental laws. Faith can then be seen as a form of reason, and reason as the faculty that conceives faith. By the same token the Christian revelation and religion fall within the necessary laws established in nature by the Creator. The incarnation and the redemption are themselves necessary in the context of the original tradition given by God: "There are, I dare say, necessary relationships derived from the laws of nature: Therefore there are laws."[10] Not only is religion, along with the family, the necessary cement of civilized society, but the very structure of the Christian church is necessary by virtue of the original tradition. In the rambling dialogues of his *Soirées de Saint-Petersbourg* (1807) and in his treatise *Du Pape* (1807) Joseph de Maistre went further: Since God is the only source of tradition, and tradition

---

[10]   *Théorie du pouvoir politique et religieux* (Paris: Collection 10.18, 1966) p. 196.

is constitutive of civilized society, the pope should be the absolute sovereign of an ecclesial theocracy, the decisions of which would carry the warrant of their own fidelity to divine tradition. The Italian theologian Gioacchino Ventura drew from these authors his understanding of tradition as a universal phenomenon that is at work in both society and the Church.

The traditionalist theories were born from reflection on the French Revolution. Yet traditionalism made an about-face when Abbé Félicité de Lamennais, though he shared de Bonald's belief in a primitive revelation, accepted some of the basic ideas of the Revolution: post-revolutionary society should be rebuilt on the basis of an alliance between the people and the pope, over against kings, emperors, and other tyrants. Traditionalism was condemned, however, when some of its implications were seen to confuse reason and faith and to make rationalism a consequence of fideism. Lamennais's "philosophy of common sense" was rejected by Gregory XVI. Likewise, the philosophy of Abbé Louis Bautain was suspect to the same pope; and Bautain, in 1835 and 1840, retracted six theses on the capacity of reason to prove the infinity of God's perfections as well as the Christian faith.[11]

Nonetheless, traditionalism was not condemned in its notion of tradition or its political theories. And echoes of it can be heard in what Leo XIII wrote about tradition. This is the case when the pope appeals to "the memory of all nations, of all centuries" (*Arcanum divinae sapientiae*), when he approves Innocent III and Honorius III for saying that the sacrament of marriage exists both "among the faithful and among the infidels," in whom, although they were "deprived of the heavenly doctrine, the nature of things, the memory of the origins, the conscience of the human race was still powerful." Leo XIII relies on Lamennais when he argues from "the judgment of all and the common sense that is the most certain voice of nature. . . ." (*Libertas praestantissimum*). The law of nature is identical with what is remembered by the memory of the origins. The universal consensus of humanity witnesses to this memory and provides a proof of nature's eternal law: "The law of nature," the pope taught, "is itself an eternal law. . . . The prince of all laws is the natural law, that is written and sculpted in the soul of each man, for it is human reason itself, commanding to do what is right and forbidding sin. . . . "

The School of Tübingen

When de Maistre or Lamennais identified the pope as the keystone of the new society, they implicitly held on to the belief that tradition is not just

---

[11]   DS, n. 2751–2756. See Walter Horton, *The Philosophy of Abbé Bautain* (New York: The University of New York Press, 1926).

a set of documentary evidence from the past, but is rather a living reality today. That traditions are living rather than static had been noted already in the fifteenth and sixteenth centuries. It had been identified as central to the Catholic faith in the polemics of the Counterreformation.[12] The theology of the school of Tübingen renovated this line of thought by closely relating the living tradition to the presence, action, and guidance of the Holy Spirit. That the Christian tradition is evolving and dynamic is made manifest by the present life of the Church.[13]

As it reacted against the classicism which, under the leadership of Napoléon, had emerged from the Revolution, the school of Tübingen tended to identify the Church's life, or the Church's consciousness, with the feelings of the believing people at large. On the one hand, this was not unrelated to the impact of the romantic mood in literature and the arts that had been illustrated in Chateaubriand's esthetic apologetics for Catholicism. The universal feeling of humanity testifies in favor of Catholic doctrine and the Catholic Church. On the other hand, when the school of Tübingen promoted the notion of a living tradition as a way out of the dilemma of Christian disunion, it echoed both Lamennais's populist dream of an alliance between the pope and the people, and the argument from universality that was dear to the traditionalists. Facing the question, "How is the multiplicity of Christian traditions compatible with the Catholic belief that the Church remains one as well as holy, catholic, and apostolic?" the school of Tübingen answered: "Only a living tradition can sort out the many traditions inherited from the past."

Yet the idea of a living tradition that is at work in the Church's self-awareness was not unambiguous. Academically the Church's self-awareness could be equated in part with the thought of the intellectuals who place their mind at the service of the Church. Pastorally it could be focused on the preaching and teaching of doctrine. Magisterially it could be seen as the source of the doctrinal and disciplinary actions by which the bishops and the pope formulate, maintain, and protect Catholic orthodoxy.

---

[12]   I have illustrated this point in *La Tradition au XVIIe siècle en France et en Angleterre* (Paris: Le Cerf, 1969). It was in the polemics of Jansenism that tradition came to be seen as a static depository of documents that illustrated the "perpetuity of the faith."

[13]   For Johann Adam Moehler the operative element of the tradition is the *sensus fidelium* or the people's Christian consciousness, in which the Holy Spirit is at work (*Die Einheit in der Kirche*, 1825). In *Symbolik* (1832), however, Moehler insisted on guidance of *sensus fidelium* by the official documents and the magisterial office as witnesses to authentic tradition. See Josef Geiselmann, *Die lebendige Überlieferung als Norm des christlichen Glaubens* (Freiburg: Herder, 1959); *Die heilige Schrift und die Tradition* (Freiburg: Herder, 1962). The theologians related to Tübingen did not all identify the life principle of tradition in quite the same way.

Newman and the Roman School

The Roman school[14] was itself sensitive to the mood of the times. It did not oppose the notion that tradition is, in the Church, living and dynamic; but it carefully inserted this dynamism in a synthesis of all the aspects of tradition that it could identify. Tradition is made of more than one strand. It is shown by its history to be a sum total of a multitude of traditions. The way in which true doctrine has been taught and learned in subsequent ages points up tradition as the predominant source of divine revelation for the faithful. The magisterium likewise has had and therefore still has a unique responsibility for the accuracy and effectiveness of the living transmission of Christian doctrine.

The theory of the development of doctrine that John Henry Newman formulated in 1845 was itself largely a product of the Romantic mind: Doctrine grows like a living organism, and, more accurately, like an idea that develops in the human mind from early vague intimations to full-fledged theory. But the suggestion that doctrinal development is analogous with a biological process was not congenial to the Roman school. For if a biological process follows the inner laws of nature given by the Creator, the transmission and the teaching of Christian doctrine draw their principle, not from nature or creation, but from the Church's guidance by the Holy Spirit. Yet the teaching of the Roman school was not far from what Newman, still an Anglican, had written in 1834: "We make, 1. a tradition interpretative of Scripture. 2. a tradition of doctrine not in Scripture. 3. a tradition of discipline, ceremonies, historical facts, etc. etc. extending to a variety of matters."[15] This was qualified by the codicil, "We consider tradition subordinate, not coordinate to Scripture," and by the accusation that Rome has invented a fourth use of Tradition as "*per se* the sufficient authority for the Church's considering a doctrine fundamental."

Toward Infallibility

Newman's analysis may not have been entirely accurate at the time, but it was prophetic. The Roman school would soon get involved in the twofold process of making tradition the absolute norm of doctrine, and the magisterium the absolute norm of tradition. From a position that was not far from

---

[14]   Walter Kasper, *Die Lehre von der Tradition in der Römischen Schule. Giovanni Perrone, Carlo Passaglia, Clemens Schrader* (Freiburg: Herder, 1962); J. P. Mackey, *The Modern Theology of Tradition* (New York: Herder and Herder, 1962); Richard Boeckler, *Der moderne römisch-katholische Traditionsbegriff. Vorgeschichte Diskussion um das Assumptio-Dogma Zweites Vatikanisches Konzil* (Göttingen: Vandenhoeck und Ruprecht, 1967).

[15]   First letter to Abbé Jager, in Louis Allen, *John Henry Newman and the Abbé Jager. A Controversy on Scripture and Tradition (1834–1836)* (London: Oxford University Press, 1976), pp. 36–37; Günter Biemer, *Newman on Tradition* (New York: Herder and Herder, 1966).

this Pius IX had concluded with the urgency of defining the role of the pope in terms of doctrinal infallibility. But this magisterial understanding of tradition opened the door to a further reduction that was effected by several neoscholastics: At the moment when it is taught with certainty the tradition becomes identical with the magisterium. In the heat of a discussion Pius IX may have said something like, *La tradizione sono io,*[16] though he never wrote it in an official document. His successor, however, would not have shrunk from the idea that he himself was the tradition. Did he not write in *Humanum genus,* as quoted above: "We are Almighty God's lieutenant on earth"?

Thus, Leo XIII's understanding of tradition blends an extreme form of the doctrine of the Roman school with the philosophy of common sense put forward by the traditionalists. Novelty is a mark of error. Catholic truth, because it is given by Christ, is already perfect at its beginning. What is true is as old as divine revelation, whether this is the primitive revelation, sundry elements of which linger in the conscience of humanity, or the final revelation given in Jesus Christ. "Whatever good," Leo wrote, "is contained in [modern] liberties is as old as the truth" (*Libertas praestantissimum*). This was exactly Joseph de Maistre's contention: Tradition is the present echo of a primitive and unchanging revelation that was made more specific in the teachings of Jesus Christ. And it was also the pope's objection to political liberalism. The liberals do not follow the tradition of humankind. They introduce liberties that are without foundation in nature: "The new that is brought in, if one seeks the truth, consists in a highly corrupt datum born of troubled times and an excessive libido for novelties." It has been invented by "impious men" who "introduce as it were a new thread in the divinely transmitted doctrine" (*Etsi nos*).

A Hidden Context

The detour we have made through Leo XIII's encyclicals to discover his notion of tradition reveals that a generally unperceived, though hardly hidden, horizon acted as background to the pope's judgment on Anglican ordinations. This was his massive rejection of everything the Reformers had ever done and said. To Leo XIII the Reformation was totally repulsive. And the motive for this radically negative judgment was no other than what the pope identified as the Reformers' ultimate responsibility for the nisus for novelty that he found at work in modern political and philosophical sects.

In the sixteenth century the Reformers were, as Leo wrote, "innovators." Their "zeal for novelty" led them to abandon the "patrimony of

---

[16]   On this point see Yves Congar, *La Tradition et les Traditions. Essai historique* (Paris: Fayard, 1960), p. 258, with note 111 on p. 291.

ancient wisdom" (*Aeterni Patris*). Indeed, the pope shared the assumption, which underlies much of nineteenth century Catholic apologetics, that "the true religion," Catholicism, "is easy to identify" (*Immortale Dei*, 1 November 1885) by virtue of its ancient pedigree and its universality. Only the clarity of its evidence has been dimmed by "those pernicious and deplorable zeals for new things that arose in the sixteenth century." The Protestants are those who "in more recent memory [than the Orthodox] were separated by turning away from the Roman Church" (*Praeclara gratulationis*).

Leo was convinced, not only that, in ecclesial matters at least, newness is evil, but also that Protestantism had inaugurated the deleterious reign of the new that flourished in the French Revolution, the poisoned fruits of which were being propagated by Liberalism and similar movements and sects. In these conditions the pope was bound to see the English Reformation as totally unjustified, and Cranmer's reform of the ritual of ordination as an unwarranted innovation. Being, as a matter of principle, opposed to the new when the old carries the seal of the Church, which is no other than the seal of the Author of all lawful authority, Leo XIII could not be favorably disposed toward the ritual of ordination of the Ordinal, that was used at the consecration of Matthew Parker.

In their effort to have Anglican ordinations recognized by the pope, Lord Halifax and Abbé Portal hardly realized that they were confronting Leo with a sixteenth-century image of what he had been tirelessly fighting since his election to the papacy, the search of his own time for *res novae*, for the new that destroys the old.

A Certain Notion of History

One may propose the hypothesis that another element, that was at work in the lingering Romantic atmosphere of the late nineteenth century, contributed to the shape of *Apostolicae curae* and to its conclusion. Some of the major historians of the times considered it to be the task of historical writing to use documentary evidence as material to build an authentic image of the past or, reversely, to reconstruct the past in imagination with the tools of rhetoric. Thus did Jules Michelet's *Histoire de France* depict the mind of the Franks and the events that were at the origin of the French nation. Like their remote predecessors, the Roman historians, they did not consider it unhistorical to place a speech in the mouth of historical personages, knowing full well that this speech was never given. Rhetoric belonged to the historical genre, and the rhetoric in question was naturally influenced by the literary models of triumphant Romanticism. The truth of history was its likelihood, as Hilaire Belloc, not so much later, would affirm clearly. And likelihood could only be interpreted according to the standards of modern culture. The rhetorical approach to academic history was only one step removed from the fictional history that made the novels of Sir Walter Scott immensely popular.

Now such a practice of the task of historians assumed that one can obtain an exact understanding, not only of the literal meaning of past documents, but also of the mind of long dead persons, and of the nature and role of past events as these were sensed by the people who lived through them. The historical works of John Henry Newman, whether on the Arians or on the Turks,[17] were not exempt from the ambition, that not one of our contemporary historians would dare to entertain, to describe the past as it truly was. The linguistic and textual sciences of our century have taught us to be less sanguine about our power to reconstruct the past.

Leo XIII of course did not attempt to reconstruct the English Reformation in imagination. Yet the style of his encyclicals lent itself to a certain type of rhetorical flourish. And indeed the arguments of *Apostolicae curae* presuppose the assumption, that was present in the historiography written in the Romantic mode, that one is able today to identify the exact intent of past events and texts. Leo XIII followed the rhetorical model of history when with no hesitation he determined the intent of Thomas Cranmer's liturgical work, the *nativa indoles ac spiritus* of the Ordinal, the meaning of the papal Bulls of Julius III and Paul IV, and the effect or non-effect of ordinations performed in England with the Ordinal. Such an approach to historical reconstruction could only confirm his personal view of reunion as a Romeward journey, and his understanding of his responsibility, as bishop of Rome, for the unity of Christians.

Leo XIII's Unionism

Leo was indeed concerned about reunion. This did not come to him late in his pontificate. It was already the reason why, having been elected in 1878, he made John Henry Newman a cardinal in 1879. The pope wanted to honor Newman as one who had found the right way to unity and had followed it. He may also have wished to make a gesture of goodwill and welcome toward the more Catholic tendencies that had come alive in the Church of England with the Oxford Movement, in the hope that these tendencies, as from his vantage point he understood them, would lead many more converts to Rome. This tallied with Leo's negative view of the Reformation and of the Churches that came from it. It was an early indication of his interest in the reunion of Christendom. But the pope could not envisage reunion otherwise than as a reversal of the Reformation. What was necessary was the final acceptance or the recovery of the authority of the Catholic Church that had been rejected

---

[17]   *The Arians of the Fourth Century*, new ed. (Westminster, MD: Christian Classics, 1968); "Lectures on the History of the Turks" (1853), in *Historical Sketches*, vol. I, new ed. (London, 1894), pp. 1–238.

in the sixteenth century, the highest instance of which resided precisely, by the will of God, in the pope himself.[18]

When therefore, following the unanimous vote of the cardinals of the Holy Office, his mind was made up about what the Ordinal really meant and what happened or did not happen at the consecration of Matthew Parker, Leo XIII could have no qualms about making his negative judgment known. He denied any value to the ordinations, the orders, and the apostolic succession of the bishops who were thus ordained. But in Leo's mind this judgment, negative as to the validity of the ordinations, was positive regarding the hope of reunion. Since he knew exactly what had happened in the sixteenth century he could not be mistaken in his conclusion, and it was a service to the Church to make it known. In *Apostolicae curae* Leo XIII made no pretense of meeting the conditions set forth by Vatican I for infallible pronouncements. The letter was not even addressed to the whole Catholic world as an encyclical to the worldwide episcopate would have been. Yet because it was made by himself as the bishop of Rome, his decision was undoubtedly, in the pope's own mind, an absolute determination of the truth. Beyond the argumentation of *Apostolicae curae* there looms the massive fact that Leo conceived of no higher authority than his own in any matter that touches Christian doctrine, ecclesiastical discipline, and moral behavior.

The Linguistic Problem

It was widely held in the theological textbooks of neoscholasticism, which Leo had himself promoted, that obedience is due to a papal decision regardless of what arguments support or oppose it. Whatever the possible deficiency of its documentation and argumentation, such a decision stands on its own as a proclamation of the truth simply by virtue of the authority of the one who promulgates it. Such an "extrinsicism" in the structure and exercise of authority was not created by neoscholasticism. It had come to the fore in the polemics of the Counterreformation, and it waxed through the nineteenth century in the ultramontane conception of authority. Reaction to it had contributed during the French Revolution to the populist measures of the Civil Constitution of the Clergy, under Gregory XVI and Leo XII to Lamennais's final rejection of papal authority, under Pius IX to the opposition of Gallican and Josephist bishops to the definition of papal infallibility. Under Pius X it would inspire the contention of some among the "modernists" that the truth of Christian dogma does not reside in their authoritative formulation but in the believers' inner spiritual experience. Pius X would

---

[18] On Leo's unionism see Etienne Fouilloux, *Les Catholiques et l'unité chrétienne du XIXe au XXe siècle. Itinéraires européens d'expression française* (Paris: Le Centurion, 1982); Giuseppe M. Croce, *La Badia Greca di Grottaferrata e la Rivista 'Roma e l'Oriente,'* 2 vol. (Vatican City: Libreria editrice vaticana, 1990).

identify this as "immanentism," and would call modernism "the sumtotal of all heresies" (Encyclical *Pascendi,* 1907).

Yet the possible excesses of an immanentist view of truth do not justify opposite, extrinsicist excesses. Truth cannot be imposed by way of authority regardless of the requirements of reason. Nor did the defeat of the opponents of infallibility at Vatican I resolve the fundamental problem. In no system of logic can a conclusion be divorced from its premises. In no form of discourse can a sentence be said to be true if it is irrevocably set in a context that appears to be false. The neoscholastic view of authority would make an exception in the case of papal statements protected by the Petrine function as universal primacy in the Church. Theological integrity, therefore, has to find its way between two principles. On the one hand the objection to proof-texting from Scripture is based on the linguistic impossibility of achieving sense apart from the entire horizon of discourse.[19] On the other, the urge to adorn a theological text with biblical verses, the meaning of which may have little relevance to what is being said, is equally based on the fact that a quotation acquires new meaning from the context in which it has been inserted.

Conclusion

As he endorsed his closest advisers' judgment on the Ordinal and issued *Apostolicae curae,* Leo XIII was trapped in the theology of tradition with which he was working. His negative decision on Anglican orders perfectly illustrates the twofold conviction that sacramental norms are set by tradition, and that it pertains to the magisterium alone, at its highest level, to discern what the tradition transmits. Not by accident did Leo XIII order the members of the Anglican orders commission to hand over their documentation without further trying to reach an agreement. Admittedly they seemed to be in an impasse, caught as they were between opposite evaluations, yet no more so than the mixed commission that was formed by John XXIII at Vatican Council II when it began to work toward the conciliar constitution *Dei Verbum.*

Pope Leo, however, felt no substantive need to obtain a consensus from his commission. By himself he could proclaim the truth. But if he extricated the commission on Anglican orders from a historical labyrinth, it was at the cost of falling into the snares of a defective theology of tradition, to say nothing of the additional cost of indefinitely delaying the reconciliation of the Churches.

---

[19]   For further discussion of this point see my volume, *La Théologie parmi les sciences humaines. De la méthode en théologie* (Paris: Beauchesne, 1975); and the article, "The Bull Unam sanctam of Boniface VIII," in P. C. Empie and Austin Murphy, eds., *Papal Primacy and the Universal Church* (Minneapolis: Augsburg, 1974) pp. 105–119.

"To the intent that these Orders may be continued": An Anglican Theology of Holy Orders[1]

STEPHEN SYKES*

Saepius officio (the Reply of the Archbishops of Canterbury and York to the letter *Apostolicae curae* of Pope Leo XIII)[2] cites the preface of the 1552 Ordinal as weighty evidence of the "intention of our Fathers . . . to keep and continue these offices which come down from the earliest times;" and complains that "this is a point on which the Pope is unduly silent." The doctrine of intention is, of course, by now exceptionally well trodden ground. Francis Clark in *Anglican Orders and Defect of Intention* (1956) claimed to have found seven different interpretations of the paragraph of AC alleging defect of intention in the conferral of holy orders within the Anglican rite. John Jay Hughes's lucid discussion of these claims (*Stewards of the Lord* [1970], Part III) is a model of its kind, concluding with the citation of the Preface to the Ordinal as one certain indication of the Church of England's intention to convey the highest degree of ministry, and therefore to intend "to do what the Church does."[3]

From an Anglican point of view, the difficulty is merely compounded if the very attempt to raise objection to the judgment of AC on Anglican orders is known in advance to be null and void by decree of AC itself.

We decree that these Letters and all things contained therein shall not be liable at any time to be impugned or objected to by reason of fault or any other defect whatsoever of subreption or obreption or of Our intention, but are and shall be always valid and in force, and shall be inviolably observed both juridically and otherwise, by all of whatsoever degree and pre-eminence; declaring null and void anything which in these matters may happen to be contrariwise attempted, whether wittingly or unwittingly, by any person of whatsoever authority or pretext, all things to the contrary notwithstanding.[4]

---

* Stephen Sykes is Bishop of Ely.

[1] I acknowledge with gratitude the help of the Reverend Dr. Jonathan Knight in the preparation of this paper. *Apostolicae curae* will be abbreviated in this essay as AC.

[2] *Answer of the Archbishops of England to the Apostolic Letter of Pope Leo XIII on English Ordinations*, in *Anglican Order* (London, SPCK, 1932), p. 49. This work will be quoted by its Latin title, *Saepius officio* (SO).

[3] J.J. Hughes, *Stewards of the Lord: A Reappraisal of Anglican Orders* (London, Sheed and Ward, 1970).

[4] AC, in *Anglican Orders*, p. 15.

48

The major use for modern theologians to consider one hundred years later may well be that of the status of self-validating utterances, that is, the issue of authority in the Church. ARCIC was truly bold when, in prescriptive not descriptive terms, it affirmed that Anglicans are entitled to assurance that acknowledgement of the universal primacy of the bishop of Rome would not involve the suppression of theological, liturgical and other traditions *which they value* or imposition of wholly alien traditions [my emphasis].[5] The value which Anglicans place upon the veridical character of the holy orders they transmit could scarcely be greater. It seems that the methodological, not the substantive issue presents the major challenge.

But modern ecumenism presents Anglicans with serious challenges to its theology of holy orders, and it is surely right for Anglicans to speak of the problems of their own traditions as clearly and openly as they can in the hearing of their Roman Catholic friends. The co-existence of a range of bilateral conversations enables a constant process of checking and reflection to take place. In relation to the theology of holy orders, Anglicans are under scrutiny in their conversations with Lutherans, the Reformed and the Methodists in a way which is relevant to the theme of intention. For it is bluntly asked whether it is true that the threefold ministry is "evident" from Apostolic times, as is claimed in classic Anglican sources. In the first section of this contribution I propose, therefore, to expound that claim, and to consider some classic Anglican interpretations of it, including the explicit revision of the claim in the 1979 *Book of Common Prayer* of the Episcopal Church of the United States of America. Then, secondly, I shall consider whether or not the reference to the "Apostles' time" is bound to entail a readiness to admit the relevance of historical-critical enquiry into the New Testament period. The third part of the paper develops the implications of the idea of intending to continue the orders of ministers "from the Apostles' time," by reference to a critical Methodist discussion of the evidence. Finally, the main points of the paper will be briefly summarised.

The Ordinal of the Church of England

It is evident unto all men diligently reading the Holy Scriptures and ancient authors that from the Apostles' time there have been these orders of Ministers in Christ's Church, Bishops, Priests and Deacons (Preface to the Ordinal, text of 1550, 1552 and 1662).

This text plainly affirms the existence throughout Christian history of three "orders of Ministers." It does not specify a precise relation between them,

---

[5]   *Authority in the Church II* (1981), para 22. The documents are collected in C. Hill and E. Yarnold (eds.), *Anglicans and Roman Catholics: The Search for Unity* (London, SPCK/CTS, 1994), pp. 69f.

nor of orders as a whole to the total life and being of the Church.[6] It affirms that the three orders have been in existence "since the Apostles' time;" which is a claim with truth conditions attached. It does not say that the orders were founded by Christ, nor that they are sacramental. It asserts that the existence of the orders is "evident;" but implicitly qualifies this assertion by noting the need for diligence in reading the sources. Finally the specified sources are said to be both the Holy Scriptures and ancient authors, it being assumed by this linkage that the testimony of the latter is relevant in corroborating or reinforcing the former.

There was in the mid-sixteenth century already a debate about the antiquity of the orders of ministry, which grew fiercer for Anglicans with the advancing of claims for the *de iure divino* status of presbyterian polity towards the end of that century. The debate took on a new form with the coming of historical biblical criticism and attempts to reconstruct the history of the early communities between the days of Jesus and the writings of St. Paul. In this new context a new apologia was required. For many Anglicans the most sophisticated defence of the historical claims of the Preface to the Ordinal was mounted by J.B. Lightfoot in an appended dissertation to his commentary on Philippians (1st edition, 1868). Entitled "The Christian Ministry;" this essay contained a detailed attempt to trace the development of the ministry from the days of the Apostles to the middle of the second century. "History;" claimed Lightfoot, "is obviously the sole upright, impartial referee;"[7] the doctrinal claims for episcopacy cannot be divorced from the historical. But such was the rigour and scrupulosity of his enquiry, he was widely understood to have undermined the traditional case for the apostolic origins of the episcopal office. In fact it is clear that he was convinced by the evidence for the view, widely held by writers of later centuries, that St. John had been active in the making of bishops in the churches of Asia Minor. He concludes:

The evidence for the early and wide extension of episcopacy throughout proconsular Asia, the scene of St. John's latest labours, may be considered irrefragable.[8]

In this sense Lightfoot is fully justified in claiming (as he did in the sixth edition of the work, 1881) that his enquiry confirmed the statement of the Ordinal. It involved a diligent search of ancient authors; it recognised a wide difference between the functions of apostle and bishop; it admitted that Gentile Christendom around the year 70 AD still showed "no distinct signs

---

[6] See F.E. Brightman, *The English Rite*, Vol. II (London, Rivingtons, 1915) for comparisons between the Prayer Books of 1550, 1552 and 1662.

[7] *St. Paul's Epistle to the Philippians*, revised text (London, Macmillan, 1878), p. 187.

[8] *Philippians*, p. 214.

of episcopal government."[9] What happened, Lightfoot argued, is that bishops were elevated out of the presbyterate to be the stable, permanent presidents of local churches. St. John brought the idea from Jerusalem to Asia Minor. Thus it may be literally traced to his time, without exaggerated claims for its institution by Christ, or for its universality.

For various reasons Lightfoot's account did not please all Anglicans, and an alternative view was speedily developed. It is as well to note this disagreement, because Lightfoot's essay is occasionally cited, more than one hundred years later, in support of emergency lay presidency. But his arguments were thoroughly and effectively challenged, in the first place by Charles Gore in *The Church and the Ministry* (1886), and subsequently with very considerable weight by R.C. Moberly in *Ministerial Priesthood.*[10] Where Lightfoot had been able to say no more than that the three-fold ministry might be traced to "Apostolical direction" and might thus be presumed to have "Divine sanction", Moberley insisted that the whole basis of ministry was none other than that of divine commission. Where Lightfoot apparently presented an episcopate evolved by elevation from a previously undifferentiated presbyterial order, Moberly vigorously defended the uninterrupted transmission of authority to ordain from the apostles themselves. The apostolate, he held, depends upon personal mission from Jesus Christ, and is the basis and background of everything in the Church, evident long before titles became fixed and clear. Lightfoot was roundly criticised for spiritualising and individualising the Christian's communion with God, in such a way as to by-pass the corporate unity of the Church; the "episcopal system" was presented as antithetical to "spirituality." By contrast Moberly insists on the bodiliness of the necessary means by which God has provided for the life of the Church, from which we have no power to dispense ourselves though God is not bound to them.

A sharper controversy, with practical relevance to the ministerial orders of the Church of India, arose in the 1940s and 50s, with the publication of *The Apostolic Ministry* (1947), a reply *The Historic Episcopate* (1954), and a reply to the reply, *This Church of Christ* (1955). Edited by Gore's successor as Bishop of Oxford, K. E. Kirk, part of the point of *The Apostolic Ministry* was to strengthen Gore's position with more detailed historical argument. The bishop, it was argued by Austin Farrer and Gregory Dix, corresponds to the Jewish *shaliach*, sent directly from God and thus the primary minister of every sacrament. There were numerous Anglican re-

---

[9] *Philippians*, p. 201.
[10] *The Church and the Ministry* (London, SPCK, 1886) was republished in a revised edition in 1919, and again in 1936. As Bishop of Birmingham Gore gave Lenten Lectures on *Orders and Unity* (London, Murray, 1909) which were motivated in part by Lightfoot's continuing influence. *Ministerial Priesthood* (London, Murray, 1897) was published with an appendix on Roman Criticism of Anglican Orders written after the publication of AC.

plies, but they were focussed in *The Historic Episcopate* (which included an essay by a young Hugh Montefiore). Historical arguments, it was pointed out, cannot achieve more than probability; and in the matter of a so-called "essential ministry" probability is not enough.

Modern Anglican New Testament scholars tend to be much more sceptical and cautious than Gore or Moberly. Reginald Fuller, for example, in a contribution to an ecumenical symposium, took the widespread view that the New Testament evidence is pluriform in character. The Pauline communities held a charismatic view of ministry; an institutionalised ministry is characteristic of the sub-apostolic age. The letters to "Timothy" and "Titus" are a midway stage en route to the monepiscopacy of the second century. Succession by ordination is a means of handing on the faith, unconnected with eucharistic presidency. Fuller cites a report of the 1930 Lambeth Conference in support of the view that the episcopate can only be justified, like the Canon of Scripture or the Creeds themselves, as the result of a "process of adaptation and growth."[11]

The appeal to "development;" of course, rings bells with Anglicans, for it was this issue that John Henry Newman made central to his case for leaving Anglicanism. Different bells ring for Roman Catholics, for "development" was alleged by Alfred Loisy to explain the startling discontinuities between the original preaching of Jesus and what the Church became. Both the theology and the life of the Church have histories; but those histories know moments when a "Yes" or a "No" was firmly stated about a "development." These moments present their own difficulties and temptations. After Nicaea it is tempting to say that all the best pre-Nicene fathers were really trinitarians. After Luther, or after the Council of Trent, after the *Book of Common Prayer* or after *Apostolicae curae* one may be informed to engage in dubious exercises of justification. Historians have the important duty of acting like investigative journalists in a democracy. Wisdom, and the love of truth, suggests we adopt a dialectical model which recognises competitive interests, and sustains the process of argument. Discussion of the historical claims of the Preface to the Anglican Ordinal of 1550, 1552, and 1662 cannot be set aside.

A certain dissatisfaction with it is evident in the careful revision of the Preface contained in the 1979 *Book of Common Prayer* of the Episcopal Church of the USA. It reads:

---

[11] "The Ministry in the New Testament," in H.J. Ryan and J.R. Wright(eds.) *Episcopalians and Roman Catholics: Can They Ever Get Together?* (Denville, Dimension, 1972), p. 103. And, he pertinently asks, if legitimate development justifies episcopacy, could it not also for Anglicans justify the primacy of the Bishop of Rome? ARCIC subsequently made both these moves (*Ministry and Ordination* (1973), para 6; see also the comment in *Elucidation* (1979), para 4; and *Authority in the Church II* (1981), para 7.

The Holy Scriptures and ancient authors made it clear that from the apostles' times, there have been different ministries within the Church. In particular, since the time of the New Testament, three distinct orders of ordained ministers have been characteristic of Christ's holy catholic Church. First . . . etc.

It is notable that the historic claim has been changed. From the Apostles' time all that is asserted (uncontroversially) is the existence of "different ministries." It is notable that the use of the word "ministry" in the Prayer Book Catechism includes lay ministries. At the same time three "distinct" orders of "ordained ministry" are said to have been "characteristic" of the Church "since the time of the New Testament." Oddly enough, and perhaps unintentionally, the historic claim is, if anything, more stringent. Although the dating is relaxed to embrace the last document of the New Testament canon, it is asserted that by that date the episcopate, presbyterate and diaconate were both distinct as orders and already characteristic of the Church. Lightfoot's defence of the Johannine origin of the episcopate, by contrast, stopped short of claiming that it was at that date characteristic of the church as such.

Both of the two Prefaces are, however, united in one feature, namely the reference to the Holy Scriptures of the New Testament, as providing evidence for the three orders of ministry which it is the Anglican intention to continue, and reverently to use and esteem. The next question to examine turns on the relationship between the use of Scriptures as doctrine, and modern critical study of biblical history.

Ministry and Scripture

In relation to the theology of the ordained ministry, the Ordinal and the Thirty-nine Articles of Religion make a series of theological and historical claims. As we have seen "from the Apostles' time" it is said there have been three orders of ministers.[12] These have been appointed by the Holy Spirit (or by Divine Providence). Scripture readings from the Epistles (1 Tim: 3), the Book of Acts (Acts 6:2–7, or 20:17–35) and the Gospels (Mt. 28:18–20, Jn. 10:1–16) demonstrate "of what dignity, and of how great importance" the offices are.[13] The ministration of Word and Sacraments are carried out in Christ's name, and with his commission and authority.[14] The work of the ministry pertains to the salvation of humankind, and can only be carried out on the basis of the study of the Holy Scriptures, by people whose life is lived according to its rule.[15] Whatever is not contained in the Scriptures could not

---

[12]   Collect for Deacons and for Priests, *Book of Common Prayer* (1662); Ordinal.
[13]   Exhoration of the Bishop, BCP (1662) Ordinal.
[14]   Article XXVI.
[15]   Exhortation of the Bishop, BCP (1662) Ordinal.

be required as a matter of belief, or thought to be necessary to salvation.[16]

The implications of this series of interlocking affirmations are far-reaching. The ordained ministry cannot be separated from the gospel of salvation, which is the point of there being the Holy Scriptures (and the Church). Therefore the interpretation of the theology of such ministry, and of all developments which it undergoes, can only be by reference to the gospel as taught in the Holy Scriptures. It is not merely what Jesus did historically which controls the trajectory of a true development. It is, rather, the soteriological (and thus christological) heart of the gospel which provides us with criteria for inspecting the validity of developments within the pattern of ministries emanating "from the apostles time." Loss of interpretative validity may plainly occur through the weakening of a grasp upon the gospel itself.

The New Testament evidence has also been very carefully considered by Roman Catholic scholars, notable among whom is Raymond Brown. In 1970 Brown published the results of his examination of biblical evidence for "the unqualified idea that the bishops are the successors of the apostles." The limitations to be placed on that claim were relevant, he believed, both to the modern practice of the episcopate and the relations with non-Catholic churches. Nonetheless the affirmation that the episcopate was divinely established or established by Christ himself

can be defended in the nuanced sense that the episcopate gradually emerged in a Church that stemmed from Christ and that this emergence was (in the eyes of faith) guided by the Holy Spirit.[17]

In a later work which pursues the implications of this middle way between a dogmatic conservatism that claims too much for history and a liberal assertion that historical uncertainty undermines the teaching authority of the church, Raymond Brown again illustrates the importance of the word "nuance." It is admitted that there is no evidence that Jesus had thought out the issue of presidency at the eucharist. But all that is required for the validity of the Tridentine dogma that Christ established the Apostles as priests with the words, "Do this in commemoration of me" (DBS 1752) is a "nuance,"

namely that establishment by Christ involves looking at what Jesus did historically on the night before he died in the light of the christology, liturgy, and ecclesiology of the next 100 years which interpreted the original actions and words.[18]

---

[16]   Article VI.
[17]   R.E. Brown, *Priest and Bishop, Biblical Reflections* (New York, Paulist Press, 1970), p. 3.
[18]   R.E. Brown, *Biblical Exegesis and Church Doctrine* (New York, Paulist Press, 1985), p. 48.

In this way "institution by Christ" is seen as not identical with "institution by Jesus." The former phrase is intended to cover developments in accordance with "God's plan in Christ."

But this is a view which itself needs to be nuanced if the possibility of a *loss* of interpretative validity is to be taken into account, as well as gain in insight. It is admitted on all sides that "development" is not, of itself, a theologically adequate category. An institution may "develop" and at the same time insight may decline. There are bound to be criteria for true development, as Newman realised, and they cannot simply consist of emphatic affirmation. It is not a case of "what I say three times is true." The grounds for authoritative declaration that a certain development is in accordance with God's will are bound to relate to the original making clear of God's will. In relation to what is said to have been "instituted by Christ" (in the sense of later emergence or development in accordance with God's plan in Christ), there must be a connection with God's will in Jesus, and that itself will have historical truth conditions attached to it.

Francis Martin offers an analogy for the development of office, in a treatment of the question with similarities to Moberly's argument. He holds that the function of offices belongs to the "intrinsic genetic code of the church," but that its manifestation at any given time needs "non-genetic (epigenetic) factors," rather as a musical score (the code) needs a company of musicians.[19] The New Testament has plenty of instances of "charisms of service," it also has "ministries," functioning on a somewhat more permanent level. But an "office" is something different (it will be observed that this sophisticated argument has the effect of excluding women from office, both in the New Testament period and subsequently). Office is "a stable ministry whose function is to secure the permanence of the apostolic teaching."

While charisms and ministries are expressions of the aspect of "otherness" inherent in the source of the Church's life, office adds to this the expression of an aspect of otherness that works within the corporeal and thus historical nature of the Church.[20]

There was a period when charisms, ministries and offices were not differentiated, as the fluidity of terminology illustrates. But all the time, working to produce a clearly differentiated office, which would defend the truth and act as an agent of encouragement, was a tendency, a "code," implicit in the Church from the first.

It is notable, of course, that a biological model is used, rather than a sociological one. The process of institution building is extremely familiar in sociological analysis, but Martin chooses to ignore it entirely. Although his

---

[19]   Francis Martin, *The Feminist Question* (Grand Rapids, Eerdmans, 1994), p. 109f.
[20]   *Ibid.*, p. 92.

model permits him to say that particular performances of the basic score may be flawed, the score itself, like the code, is simply a given. While a convincing account can be offered of the period of variety, when the terminology for charisms and ministries was fluid and "office" scarcely perceptible as a structural feature, nonetheless in developmental terms "it," that is the true identity of office, was bound to emerge: In effect there was no risk, other than delay; and above all no cost in the development, other than occasional malperformance.

It is instructive to discover that the implication of the riskiness of historical-critical enquiry had already been robustly faced by the Lambeth fathers in 1897. In their encyclical they wrote:

The critical study of the Bible by competent scholars is essential to the maintenance in the Church of a healthy faith. That faith is already in serious danger which refuses to face questions that may be raised either on the authority or genuineness of any part of the Scriptures that have come down to us. . . . A faith which is always or often attended by a secret fear that we dare not inquire less inquiry should lead us to results inconsistent with what we believe, is already infected with a disease which may soon destroy it.[21]

Inquiry into the form which ministry took in the New Testament period is, indeed, historical inquiry, and its conclusions cannot be presumed. Did Jesus envisage a continuous life of the Church, extending through the centuries and showing no sign of coming to an end? Did he contemplate merely a short period in which his followers would simply wait for the climax of history? The questions have been posed since the days of Weiss and Schweitzer and the evidence denies us certitude, pointing us rather to the implications of Jesus' teaching and response to suffering. The case seems rather that Jesus anticipates a covenantal crisis between God and humanity, and presents his own ministry, teaching and life as a sign and agent of the breaking-in of the new age, the kingdom of God.

That the teaching and the events of Jesus' life provoked a whole series of interpretative puzzles, is the overwhelming evidence of the New Testament Scriptures. Though the new communities of disciples saw themselves as a new race of people, they had huge tasks of improvisation to undertake. What held them together, if at all, was a grasp upon the gracious love of God's action in Jesus Christ, which demanded of them grace, mutual forgiveness, love and a constant quest for unity. The unity of the churches of the New Testament period is only ever a relative unity within a plurality of interpretative enterprises, focussed upon God's new justifying act of Christ.

The theology of an ordained ministry, therefore, needs the historical-critical inquiry into the New Testament because it is in constant danger of

---

[21] *The Five Lambeth Conferences* (London, SPCK, 1920), pp. 188f.

forgetting both the fact of variety and the source of the unity. Of course there were boundaries to that variety, as the new communities defined themselves over against Judaism and various forms of gnosticism or error. The process illustrated by the Johannine communities (on Raymond Brown's reconstruction of their interaction) suggests a constant process of interpretation and reinterpretation, in the course of which, as the Johannine letters show, it is not unreasonable to think that various forms of sectarian myopia developed inside the allegedly canonical group.[22] Boundaries might be drawn too tightly, under sectarian pressures, as well as too laxly under the normal processes of compromise.

Nonetheless, although the New Testament itself is evidence of the fluidity of the early situation, it does not constitute grounds for the legitimation of the rival denominationalism of the modern churches. On the contrary. Lazy tolerance of institutionalised diversity is denied by the New Testament evidence about the urgency of the quest for unity between fellow members of Christ's one body. In this case it is the theology of the New Testament which is determinative, the pluriform witness of the leading blocks of New Testament material to the significance of the life, death and resurrection of Jesus Christ, as God's reconciling act between Jew and Gentile, male and female, slave and freeperson.

Intending "the Orders"

Formally speaking it is said that the doctrine of intention expressed in AC does not differ from that advanced by Richard Hooker in Book V of the *Laws of Ecclesiastical Polity*. Here, he quotes the canonist Lancelot to the effect that:

> the known intent of the Church generally doth suffice, and, where the contrary is not manifest, we may presume that he which outwardly doth the work, hath inwardly the purpose of the Church of God.[23]

The point of AC is to challenge the claim that the Anglican rite "outwardly doth the work" on the grounds that the rite has been changed with the intention of "rejecting what the Church does, and what by the institution of Christ belongs to the nature of the Sacrament" (AC 9).

Saepius officio, as one would expect, repeatedly returns to the Scriptural justification for the Anglican rite, denying that there is consistency in medieval ordinals and that it is appropriate to use medieval and later customs as the standard of what the Church does (VIII). Thus "our Fathers'

---

[22] R.E. Brown, *The Community of the Beloved Disciple* (New York, Paulist, 1979).
[23] *Laws*, Bk 5, para 58. See the helpful review article by T.A. Lacey, "Intention;" *Hastings Encyclopaedia of Religion and Ethics*, Vol. 7 (Edinburgh, Clark, 1914), pp. 380–2.

fundamental principle was to refer everything to the authority of the Lord, revealed in the Holy Scriptures" (XVIII); they wished to return "to the simplicity of the Gospel" (XIX); they "aimed at simplicity" and "followed without doubt the example of our Lord and His Apostles" (XIX). The whole document's position on priesthood is said to be the result of "taking our stand on Holy Scripture" (XIX) and in the closing peroration the Pope is invited to weigh patiently "what Christ intended when he established the ministry of His Gospel" (XX). In this reply, therefore, it is not possible to separate the Anglican understanding of holy orders from the scriptural witness.

This position is consistent with the reference in the preface to the Ordinal to "these orders," meaning the three orders of ministers, Bishops, Priests and Deacons "from the Apostles' time:" It is these which the Church of England intends to continue, reverently to use and esteem. In the light of what we have seen to be the tentative and plural solutions to the matter of leadership in the New Testament communities, how convincing is this "stand" on Holy Scripture?

There is some evidence that more recent ecumenical theology has found it attractive to qualify the position. Building on some notable work on Tradition in the 1970s, ARCIC I made central the gift of the Holy Spirit to the apostolic community, and by implication the continuity between the initial mission, the written record and the later life of the people of God. Objection was raised to the adequacy of its description of the Scriptures as "a normative record of the authentic foundation of the faith." This, it was held, made it possible for ARCIC "to treat certain developments as possessing an authority comparable to that of Scripture itself." The subsequent Elucidation is more strongly christological than the original text:

> The person and work of Jesus Christ, preached by the apostles and set forth and interpreted in the New Testament writings, through the inspiration of the Holy Spirit, are the primary norm for Christian faith and life. Jesus, as the Word of God, sums up in himself the whole of God's self-disclosure. The Church's essential task, therefore, in the exercise of its teaching office, is to unfold the full extent and implications of the mystery of Christ, under the guidance of the risen Lord.
>
> No endeavour of the Church to express the truth can add to the revelation already given. Moreover, since the Scriptures are a uniquely inspired witness to divine revelation, the Church's expression of that revelation must be tested by its consonance with Scripture.[24]

Given that christology is inescapably a soteriological discipline, this explanation is all one could wish. The Anglican argument about the theology of orders is that ordained ministry is inseparable from God's self-disclosure in

---

[24]   *Elucidation* (1981), para. 2.

Jesus Christ, and that the Church's expression of the meaning of ordination must relate to Jesus Christ and be tested by its consonance with Scripture. Moreover because it is *Jesus* Christ to whom reference is made, the disciplines of historical enquiry are plainly relevant in testing the authority and genuineness of the traditions contained in the text.

As the ARCIC elucidation indicates, the position which makes a strong affirmation of the person and work of Christ as the "primary norm" for Christian faith and life is under no obligation to deny the guidance of the Holy Spirit in the subsequent life of the Church. ARCIC-I goes on to point out that there are weaker and stronger versions of this affirmation of the continuing influence of the Holy Spirit, and a certain tension between them. No doubt the theology of holy orders is itself caught within these tensions both between and within the Roman Catholic and Anglican Churches. But the real frontier for ecumenical work lies between those who take an affirmative view of the structures of ordained ministry in relation to the service of the gospel, and those who see in them a matter for suspicion, as potential or actual forms of bondage or as *adiaphora* in the life of the Church. Because the latter often present themselves as occupying the high ground of scriptural authority or of scholarly enquiry into the early communities, agreement between Anglicans and Roman Catholics in relation to the christological norm for a theology of holy orders is of great importance.

What therefore can be said today about the "stand" of the archbishops upon Scripture? It is, of course, challenged. One eloquent and effective critic has been the distinguished Methodist New Testament scholar and churchman, Kingsley Barrett. In *The Signs of an Apostle* (1970) and *Church, Ministry and Sacraments* (1985),[25] Barrett has expounded a widely-held and influential perspective on the ministry in the New Testament Churches, in contrast to that which he attributes to episcopalians of all kinds. He does not exaggerate when in the latter work, he accepts "a fair measure of responsibility for the failure of schemes to unite the Church of England and the Methodist Church" (p. 7), though the arguments he uses are common to a wide range of non-episcopalian biblical scholars.

The questions to which Barrett strives to give an answer are: What are the marks by which the true, authentic church of Christ may be discerned? What characteristics distinguish its faith and order? From the examination of the New Testament evidence the answer cannot consist, he holds, in any simple formula. There were no canons of orthodoxy in Paul's day, no observable proofs of his apostolicity in such a way as to demonstrate his status to an impartial observer. Of Jesus himself, the same is true, "the fact is he

---

[25]   C.K. Barrett, *The Signs of An Apostle* (London, Epworth, 1970); and *Church, Ministry and Sacraments in the New Testament* (Exeter, Paternoster, 1985).

was content to go on doing the task he had received from the Father, without concerning himself over the questions of status."[26]

This fact is immediately used by Barrett to deny the possibility of attempting to look for infallible and unmistakable marks of apostolicity in the church:

A church order that claims to represent the one true apostolic form of the church will not only fail to do justice to the variety found in the New Testament, it will run the risk of being more apostolic than the apostles, or, more accurately, will be seen to adopt an attitude from which the apostles had to be drawn away. The church lives by faith, not by its own form, and the seal of its apostolicity is to be found not in its order but in the sinners it has won from wickedness to God, and in the needy it has comforted, healed and helped.[27]

Footnoted references here demonstrate how seriously Barrett takes the Methodist Conference affirmation of 1746 that there is no determinate plan of church government appointed in Scripture, and Wesley's abhorrence of church rules excluding the baptised from worshipping God together. There are, nonetheless, marks of apostolicity and a proper exercise of authority within the Church. Barrett recognises that in the course of opposition to Gnosticism Christians developed "orthodoxy" and a ministry of authorised teachers. But even then the seeds of a disastrous legalism were sown, until the "theology of glory" was challenged at the reformation by a "theology of the cross." Now the Church is able more clearly to live with a dialectical relation to apostolic authority, on the one hand submitting to the original testimony, and to the apostles who transmitted and guaranteed it; on the other living in freedom, not in a new form of bondage.

Exercising this freedom Barrett clearly designates the developments of Ignatius' time as authoritarian, and "part of a quest for security, a flight from the dangerous *sola fide* of the New Testament."[28] He draws a striking contrast between Paul's use of the word "guarantee" in 2 Cor. 1:21 ("he who guarantees [*bebaion*] us . . . is God"), and in Smyrneans 8:2 ("Whatever the bishop shall approve, is well pleasing to God; that everything which you do may be sure and valid [*bebaion*])."[29] In the new atmosphere there is, he holds, a deficiency of theological criticism based on the crucified and risen Lord. Barrett sees the church as embraced by a paradox, of its being at once central in the purpose of God, but also, and at the same time, peripheral. "It is not that there are some bits of the church that are vital and some that are unessential; every bit shares the twofold character of the whole."[30]

---

[26] *Signs of an Apostle,* p. 87.
[27] *Ibid.,* p. 88.
[28] *Church, Ministry and Sacraments,* p. 97.
[29] *Ibid.,* p. 98.
[30] *Ibid.,* p. 26.

The reply to this argument cannot, I believe, rest on asserting the illegitimacy of the theological criticism of Ignatius. It seems to me futile to deny that in its developing institutionalisation the Church paid costs, as well as reaped advantages. This would be my reply to Martin. There is no original "genetic code" or "score" whose perfection can simply be asserted, and which is awaiting the appropriate conditions of realisation or performance. What we have is an historic process with a combination of advantages and drawbacks. If what occurred by the middle of the second century is baptised (as it were) by the phrase "instituted by Christ," the legitimation of having in the development of offices a "divine institution" precludes the normal exercise of drawing attention to the negative consequence of the development itself. Barrett quite properly resists this tactic and his opposition is signalled in his constant objection to terms like "security," "guarantee," "infallible," "unmistakable," and "proof." There is, perhaps, a theological gulf to cross here from both sides, by those who cannot conceive how a "providential" development could be vitiated by attendant drawbacks, and by those whose attention is so caught by the negative features that they infer the process to be itself a decline.

Barrett's position is more vulnerable, it seems to me, on the score of sociological unrealism, and subsequent Pauline scholarship has been readier to use the available techniques. The goal of unity pursued by the sub-apostolic and later churches was undoubtedly Pauline and biblical. We do Ignatius and later writers no service by abstracting their texts from their concrete situations. They, of course, legitimated their solutions to the problems of authority in a voluntary society pursuing unity, by over-inflated claims. We have no obligation to endorse them in exactly their terms. But it sounds odd in the light of both Gospels and Epistles to accuse them of a uniquely deplorable "authoritarianism." Nor, on the other hand, need we pretend that Ignatius or the author of 1 Clement, or indeed most second century writers, achieved anything like the dialectical subtlety of the theology of Paul.

In one important respect Barrett's interpretation of the New Testament evidence is an advance on some of the standard ways of construing the growth of institution and structures. Where Lutheran (and some Anglican) writers have resorted to a sharp distinction between matters essential to the Church and mere *adiaphora*, Barrett explicitly states that every part of the church shares in the "paradox" of being at once central and peripheral. The question at once arises whether he would be prepared to say this of the procedures and disciplines required to keep a united ordained ministry in the church. Or would it be, paradoxically, essential to his view of the church that no structure of *any* kind could be allowed the task of preserving unity? This latter stance is familiar to Anglicans from some modern ecumenical discussions in which it is required of them that they declare the episcopate to be *adiaphoron,* as a pre-condition of re-establishing unity. If Barrett, however, were to allow that Anglicans might embrace what he calls the paradox of centrality and peripherality specifically of the episcopate, then new ecumenical consequences might follow. The judgement of *Church and Justification,* the Lutheran-Roman Catholic document, that there is no fundamental conflict or even opposition between justification and the Church contains the seeds of this view. As the Commission states, from the standpoint of the doctrine of justification it is possible that "all the church's institutions, in their self-understanding and exercise, contribute to the church's abiding in the truth of the gospel which alone in the Holy Spirit creates and sustains the church."[31]

Conclusion

In this paper I have drawn attention to the problem of intending to continue the orders of ministry from the apostles' time. There can be no serious doubt that the Church of England adopted an Ordinal which they believed embodied that intention. To validate the claim of the Preface to the Ordinal is to make both an historical, and a theological claim. The historical claim depends on what is meant by an "office," and my paper does not attempt to adjudicate on the evidence which is differently evaluated. The theological claim, however, is also unavoidable. It means getting the place of office in due relation to the mystery of Christ's atoning work. If the content and significance of the gospel of justifying grace to be received by faith were to be distorted, then whatever "office" had become in the course of time, it would cease to be able to claim to be orders from the apostles' time. The New Testament remains the touchstone for an appropriate christological and soteriological "placing" of the significance of office in the Church.

    In this paper I have attempted to steer a *via media* between, on the one hand, simply legitimating the developments of office in the Church, and, on the other hand, of dismissing them as evidence of a decline into authoritarianism. The institutionalisation of the Church imposes costs at the same time as it bestows benefits. This development is neither simply good news, nor bad; it is ambivalent. From now on a very careful eye has to be kept upon the potential for the abuse of power inherent in office.[32]

    The Anglican discussion of AC and SO is obliged to take serious account of all the ecumenical dialogues in which Anglicans are involved, not

---

[31] Lutheran-Roman Catholic Joint Commission, *Church and Justification* (Geneva, Lutheran World Federation, 1994).

[32] See further, Stephen Sykes' "Episcopé and Power in the Church," in Bruce D. Marshall (ed.) *Theology and Dialogue, Essays in Conversation with George Lindbeck* (Notre Dame, Notre Dame University Press, 1990), pp. 191–212; reprinted in *Unashamed Anglicanism* (London, Darton, Longman and Todd, 1995), pp. 178–198.

least because Roman Catholics are involved in them too. To a considerable extent the negativity of AC is a methodological problem, the lines of whose resolution, though by no means easy, are increasingly apparent. SO, on the other hand, still needs and deserves elucidation, not just in the effectiveness of its historical argument, but in its relation to the theological stance upon Scripture. Here the ecumenical argument is still exceptionally open, lively and important. To recognise ambivalence in the development of office has the potential to locate it more profoundly within a Church focussed not upon human beings, but upon Christ and his atonement.

A New Context: ARCIC and Afterwards

EDWARD YARNOLD*

ARCIC-I, in their agreed statement on ministry and ordination, did not claim to have reached agreement on the validity of Anglican orders, but they did claim to have set the question in a new context, which might make solution possible.[1] Thus the commission proposed a strategic option in the search for a solution which would not require either Church to admit it had been in error. If the search was successful, Roman Catholics would not need to concede that *Apostolicae curae* had been mistaken and that Anglican orders had been valid in 1896, nor would Anglicans need to concede that their judgment had been mistaken, and that their orders were invalid in 1896. ARCIC habitually saw its task as the uncovering of agreement already existing between the Churches, not the negotiation of a change in the doctrine of either Church. In view of Rome's habitual reluctance to reverse even those doctrinal decisions for which infallibility is not claimed, there seemed to be good reasons in favour of this option. Ecumenical dialogue at this level is the art of the possible.

There are, to be sure, some aspects of *Apostolicae curae* which seem to invite the test of a direct attack: e.g. its interpretation of the intention to do what the Church does, its assertion that the form of the Edwardine Ordinal was insufficient when judged in its sixteenth-century context, its interpretation of earlier judgments which Rome had passed on Anglican orders, and, some might say, its understanding of validity and of apostolic succession. Moreover, it has been shown that Leo's use of such terms as "irreformable" need not be taken quite at its face value, as he had already employed language no less strong in asserting a matter of no doctrinal relevance at all, namely the authenticity of the tomb of St. James at Compostella.[2] Nevertheless it is not my intention to consider whether ARCIC-I's strategic choice was wise, or whether some other strategy might prove more successful. My more modest aim is simply to suggest ways in which the context within which Anglican orders should be evaluated has changed still further since the publication of *The Final Report* in 1982.

---

* Edward J. Yarnold, S.J., is Research Lecturer at Oxford University, and he has been a member of the first and second Anglican-Roman Catholic International Commissions.
[1] *Final Report*, Ministry, Elucidation 6.
[2] See J. Russell and O. Rafferty, "St. James the Great and Anglican Orders," *Heythrop Journal* 27 (1986), pp. 178–80.

1982 also saw the meeting between Pope John Paul II and Archbishop Robert Runcie at Canterbury, at which they announced the formation of ARCIC-II, and placed on the new commission's agenda the study of "all that hinders the mutual recognition of the ministries of our two Communions." After ARCIC-II had made a first, rather fruitless, attempt at tackling this problem, Cardinal Willebrands, then President of the Pontifical Council for Christian Unity, gave a new impetus and direction to the investigation in a letter to the commission's Co-Chairmen dated 13 July 1985.[3] Indicating that the condemnation of 1896 "rested above all on what he [Leo XIII] described as the *nativa indoles ac spiritus* (native character and spirit) of the [Anglican] Ordinal as a whole," which was said to make the form and intention defective in the context of the Ordinal, even if they might be adequate in another context, the cardinal suggested that acceptance of *The Final Report* by both Communions would provide the new context of which the Commission had spoken, and would show that this native character of the Anglican rites might no longer be open to the criticisms which Pope Leo had made against it. He therefore suggested that Anglican Ordinals currently in use should be analysed to see if, in such a new context, they could now be evaluated more positively than the Edwardine Ordinal had been evaluated in 1896. Cardinal Willebrands further observed that, although the "continuity in the apostolic succession of the ordaining bishop" was a separate problem requiring a different solution, the "explicit profession of one faith in Eucharist and Ministry" would be "the strongest possible stimulus" to the discovery of such a solution.

Following the cardinal's suggestion, English ARC, on behalf of the International Commission, set up a sub-commission, which examined the *Book of Common Prayer,* Alternative Service Book and Roman Catholic rites of ordination, and, in an unpublished report, concluded that, with the exception of the BCP rite for the ordination of a deacon, the three ordinals corresponded to the understanding of the Eucharist and the priesthood expressed in *The Final Report* of ARCIC-I. It did not, however, consider means of repairing any breach in the apostolic succession which might be considered to exist.

In addition ARCIC-II had hopes for another means of solving the problem. Its strongest reason for spending several years over a document on "The Church as Communion" was the hope that ecclesial agreement on the basis of *koinonia* would make it easier to solve outstanding problems, including that of the recognition of orders. However, that hope has not yet been fulfilled. The document, when eventually published in 1991, could go no further than stating that:

---

[3]   See *Anglican Orders—A New Context* (London: CTS, 1986).

An appreciation both of the existing degree of communion between Anglicans and Roman Catholics as well as the complete ecclesial communion to which we are called will provide a context for the discussion of the long-standing problem of the reconciliation of ministries which forms part of ARCIC-II's mandate (n. 57).

We shall see later, however, that ARCIC-II was in some quarters believed to have achieved more agreement than this.

I shall consider three ways in which the context has changed since 1982: (1) The official responses by both churches to ARCIC's claim to have reached substantial agreement, i.e. agreement on essentials, concerning Eucharist and ministry; (2) new developments regarding the understanding of apostolic succession; (3) the imposition by the Vatican of new, more stringent criteria for the acceptance of the validity of orders.

Substantial agreement?

Cardinal Willebrands was careful not to preempt the decision of the two churches as to whether agreement on essentials had indeed been reached. Recalling the reservations expressed by the Congregation for the Doctrine of the Faith in 1982, he indicated that he expected "various calls for further study or further discussion on aspects of the Report," which he hoped would lead to "greater clarity and to a deepening of shared faith and of mutual assurance." In the event, both sides in their respective responses voiced certain misgivings, although these were much stronger on the Roman Catholic side. Although the resolution passed at the 1988 Lambeth Conference affirmed that the statements on Eucharist and Ministry, together with their Elucidations, were "consonant in substance with the faith of Anglicans," the appended Explanatory Note showed that Anglican approval was not universal: there were said to be "continuing anxieties" among some Anglicans in the area of eucharistic sacrifice and presence, while "some Provinces asked for a clarification of 'priesthood.'" The Roman Catholic Official Response in its final summary expressed its verdict in terms that were not dissimilar to the Anglican note, indicating areas "about which further study or clarification is required before it can be said that the Statements made in the Final Report correspond fully to Catholic doctrine on the Eucharist and on Ordained Ministry." What makes the Roman Catholic Response so different from the Anglican is the detail with which the request for clarification is made, and the insistence on "*identity* of the various statements with the faith of the [RC] church" (n. 33, my italics). ARCIC-II tried to meet this Vatican plea for further study by formulating in 1993 "Requested Clarifications on Eucharist and Ministry," which Cardinal Cassidy, who succeeded Cardinal Willebrands as President of the Pontifical Council for the Unity of Christians, judged to have "greatly strengthened" the statements on Eucharist and Ministry, so that "no further study would seem to be required at this stage." Lest we should be tempted to conclude that as a result the churches are now in a position to make the common declaration of faith in the Eucharist and ordained ministry which Cardinal Willebrands was looking for, due weight should be given to the last three words of this judgment. Moreover, on the Anglican side the clarifications might well upset the delicate balance of *The Final Report* which made it acceptable to many Evangelical as well as Anglo-Catholic commentators.

Some critics have argued that the quest for utterly unambiguous statements of agreement is impossible of fulfilment. The Anglican-Roman Catholic Consultation in the USA dug deeply into this problem in their examination of the Lambeth and Vatican responses to ARCIC-I.[4] How can one be certain, they ask, that even within the Roman Catholic Church the faith of all the members is identical?

We pray the creed together Sunday after Sunday, and as we recite the words of the creed, we assume that the persons surrounding us intend substantially the same as we do. But on what grounds do we make this assumption? (n. 28)

They observe too that the Roman Catholic Church has joined in declarations of common faith with other churches without insisting on univocal doctrinal formulas, notably with various oriental churches which reject the Chalcedonian formula of the two natures of Christ. The U.S. document quotes an agreed statement made in 1984 by Pope John Paul and the Syrian Orthodox Patriarch Zakka I, which affirms that:

The confusion and schisms that occurred between their Churches in the later centuries . . . in no way affect or touch the substance of their faith, since these arose only because of differences in terminology and culture and in the various formulae adopted by different schools to express the same matter.

This reminds the Americans of Pope John XXIII's controversial statement at the opening of Vatican II that "the substance of the ancient deposit of the faith is one thing, and the way in which it is presented is another." But, they argue:

It is highly problematic to claim that one can distinguish the substance of the faith from the culturally determined language of its expression. How does one discern the substance beneath the words save through the words? (n. 32)

---

[4]   Included in *Anglicans and Roman Catholics: the Search for Unity* eds. C. Hill and E. Yarnold (London, SPCK/CTS, 1994), pp. 186–197.

The U.S. statement suggests two answers. The first is an appeal to "orthopraxy" as a test of orthodoxy: i.e. authentic Christian life indicates authentic Christian belief. The second appeals to experience: "shared life may make differing doctrinal formulae intelligible and reveal them to be compatible and even identical in intent" (n. 33).

However we seem to have come ominously close to Catch 22. Authentic Christian life, by virtue of which Catholics and Orthodox are joined in what Vatican II calls a "very close relationship," must, according to the Vatican II Decree on Ecumenism, include possession of "true sacraments, above all—by apostolic succession—the priesthood and the Eucharist" (UR 15). The Decree praises the Orthodox churches for the possession of these gifts, whereas the Anglican Communion is included in the judgment passed on the "separated churches and ecclesial communities in the West," which, "especially because of the lack of the sacrament of orders . . . have not preserved the genuine and total reality of the Eucharistic mystery" (UR 22). It appears that only if orthopraxy includes valid ministry can it be appealed to as a proof of the orthodox doctrine needed to establish the sufficiency of the ordination rite. Catch 22!

Apostolic Succession

In the last couple of years another factor in the equation has changed, namely the understanding of ordination in the apostolic succession.

One development in this area concerns the agreement reached in 1992 at Porvoo in Finland between the Anglican churches of England, Scotland, Wales and Ireland on the one side and the Nordic and Baltic Lutheran churches on the other.[5] One thing which all these Lutheran churches have in common is the possession of superintendent ministers to whom the name "bishop" is given. The agreement, if endorsed by the churches concerned, will involve the mutual recognition of ministries, to be followed by the participation of Anglican bishops at future Lutheran episcopal ordinations, and *vice versa*. The recognition presents no special theological problems with regard to most of the churches, for they possess an episcopate which is in direct descent from the bishops of the pre-Reformation church. In Denmark, Norway and Iceland, however, the episcopal succession was broken, as the succession was maintained only through the German Lutheran superintendent presbyter Bugenhagen, who filled the gap by consecrating a new set of bishops.

The mutual recognition of episcopates agreed at Porvoo was not dependent upon the exchange of bishops at future ordinations, for this is to

---

[5]   *Together in Mission and Ministry* (London, Church House Publishing, 1993).

take place *after* the recognition. Anglican documentation justified this decision on two grounds. The first is that "the primary manifestation of apostolic succession is in the apostolic tradition of the Church as a whole." The continuity of the ministry of oversight (i.e. episcopacy) "is to be understood within the continuity of the apostolic life and mission of the whole Church." Therefore, although the episcopal office is an important "visible sign expressing and serving the Church's unity and continuity in apostolic life, mission, and ministry," and the historic succession of bishops is "a visible and personal way of *focusing* the apostolicity of the whole Church," the apostolic succession can survive a break in the line of bishops. The second justification is that authentic episcopal ministry may be acknowledged in a church which has "preserved continuity in the episcopal office by an occasional priestly/presbyteral ordination." In that case there would be no breach in the succession which needed repairing.

Now these two lines of justification are not without precedent. St. Jerome maintained that up to the third century it was the practice at Alexandria for a presbyter to be ordained bishop by a group of fellow-presbyters, while there are well documented examples in the middle ages of presbyteral ordinations performed by abbots or by presbyters in the missions. However, both these practices came to be excluded by ecumenical councils. As for episcopal ordinations, the fourth canon of the Council of Nicaea required them to be performed by three bishops. It is perhaps true that the Council of Florence envisaged the ordination of presbyters by presbyters, for it stated that the bishop is the "ordinary" minister of the sacrament of Holy Order, thus appearing to allow for extraordinary ministers who were not bishops; subsequently however non-episcopal acts of ordination were ruled out by the decision of the Council of Trent that the sole minister of the sacrament is the bishop.

The Porvoo recommendation bears similarities with the recommendation of the unofficial Dombes Group of French Catholic and Protestant ecumenists, though there are important differences. Unlike the northern Lutheran churches, the Protestant churches represented at Dombes were non-episcopal. Like Porvoo, Dombes claimed that where apostolic faith is preserved, God will grant a ministry of word and sacrament. The Catholic participants subscribed to this view tentatively, like one throwing a bottle into the sea, as one member put it, but required such a non-episcopal church to be linked with "the normal sign of episcopal succession."[6] There is however in Dombes no suggestion that recognition of orders could *precede* the restoration of this normal sign.

Anglican advocates of the Porvoo agreement have argued that it is consistent with ARCIC's understanding of apostolic succession, or even that

---

[6]   "Pour une réconciliation des ministères," Taizé, 1973, n. 40.

it is supported by the findings of that commission. In fact ARCIC, while placing continuity of episcopal ordination within the continuity of apostolic faith and life, never suggested that the latter continuity could supply for the absence of the former. The dialogue between Catholics and Orthodox has taken the same view. In fact the Vatican Response to *The Final Report* required the necessity of episcopal ordination to be stated more clearly—a request which the Clarification by ARCIC-II tried to meet by stating that "each episcopal ordination is part of a successive line which links the bishops of today with the apostolic ministry."[7] We seem to have here an example of the danger inherent in bilateral dialogues, that the ecumenical left hand may not know (or may ignore) what the right is doing.

Another shift in the context with regard to apostolic succession has taken place in recent months on the Catholic side. It concerns the third question raised by Cardinal Willebrands, namely "the question of the continuity in the apostolic succession of the ordaining bishop." Some Catholic ecumenical well-wishers thought that the best hope for the recognition of Anglican orders lay in showing that this question could be answered favourably in many cases because of the part that had been played in Anglican episcopal ordinations by bishops whose orders were not held in doubt by the Catholic church, particularly those of the Old Catholic Church. This line of approach has an attraction especially for the more traditionally minded ecumenist. An unpublished dossier by Timothy Dufort showed that for several decades all the present bishops of the Church of England included an Old Catholic bishop in their pedigree; consequently all but the oldest priests of that church possess orders in continuity with the medieval church.

Many theologians object to the search for a solution along these lines on the grounds that it presupposes a crude "pipeline" view of apostolic succession. This dangerous slogan, however, obscures as much as it clarifies. It is indeed true that it would be crassly materialistic to envisage apostolic succession as an unbroken chain of physical contact between ordainer and ordained reaching back to one of the apostles—like a congregation holding hands at the Lord's Prayer. It would also be wrong to separate a succession of ordinations from its context within the church's life. A sane view of episcopal succession does not require one to concede validity to indiscriminate ordinations conferred by and on unattached dilettanti. To insist that ecclesial succession needs to be focused in episcopal continuity is to insist, not on an unbroken chain of physical contact, but on two other essential principles: first, that ordination is not simply the bestowal of authority, but a sacrament, which needs a properly empowered minister; secondly, that even when ordination is considered as the bestowal of authority, that au-

---

[7] C. Hill and E. Yarnold, *op. cit.*, p. 205.

thority is not conferred by the people in an ecclesial version of a social contract, but comes from Christ through the apostles.

Paradoxically, the appeal to Old Catholic participation, which more conservative Catholic ecumenists find attractive, meets with the disapproval of more radical ecumenists in both churches. For such a reliance on valid orders coming from another church seems to them in principle no different from recourse to *episcopi vagantes;* it would show unacceptable disrespect to the Anglican Communion if its orders were thought to be indebted to an extraneous body for their validity. This objection, however, loses its force when it is remembered that the Old Catholic succession is not extraneous to the Anglican Communion, for the two churches have been in communion (or "full intercommunion," as it was put in the ecumenical language in use at the time) since the thirties.

The question whether the Old Catholic participation had mended the breach in the succession indicated by *Apostolicae curae* came to the fore in the case of the conditional ordination of Dr. Graham Leonard, the former Anglican Bishop of London. Hopes had been held in some quarters that the Old Catholic factor would make it possible for the Roman Catholic Church to recognise the validity of the orders he had received, for although he did not himself have an Old Catholic co-consecrator, he was in that succession at only one or two removes. Rome however judged that Leo XIII's verdict on the insufficiency of the form and matter of the rite of the Church of England still held good. Although the full text of the deliberations on Dr. Leonard has not been published, Fr. Michael Jackson has given an author-itative account of them in *The Tablet*.[8] According to Fr. Jackson, the Roman verdict was that:

the clarifications achieved through the work of ARCIC on Eucharist and Ministry have not . . . yet proved to be sufficient grounds for verifying such a change in the *nativa indoles ac spiritus* of the Anglican Ordinal.

The word "clarifications" suggests that the judgment took account of ARCIC-II's Clarifications, and found them unconvincing. Perhaps a crumb of comfort can be gathered from the words "not yet," which leave open the possibility of a more favourable verdict in the future.

The conclusion that was drawn was not that it was still uncertain whether the language of the Anglican ordinals carried a satisfactory sense—for if so, *conditional* ordination would have been appropriate in every case—but rather that the inherent character of the ordinals was still certainly insufficient, so that normally ex-Anglican clergy would have to be ordained *absolutely*. However, in Dr. Leonard's case an exception was made because,

---

[8]   30 April 1994.

apart from his claim to apostolic succession through the Old Catholic line, there existed documentary evidence of two other factors: first, of his "Catholic intention at his priestly and episcopal ordinations," and of his "profoundly Catholic theology"; secondly, of the intention of the Anglican bishops of Old Catholic lineage who ordained him priest and bishop, and of the actions and words they employed. These factors were considered sufficient to change the inherent character of the Ordinal, so as to create prudent doubt about the invalidity of his orders, thus making conditional rather than absolute ordination the correct procedure in his case.[9]

While welcoming this judgment, I am not convinced about the underlying logic, because to say that the *nativa indoles ac spiritus* was changed *in this particular instance* seems a contradiction in terms: what is *"nativa"* is independent of the particular circumstances of a particular case. We are left with the conclusion that in the eyes of the Vatican one of two conditions will need to be fulfilled if Old Catholic participation can validate orders today: (1) if one of the ordaining bishops is himself an Old Catholic or a member of another church whose orders the Vatican accepts, there must be documentary proof of his intention and the form he used; (2) if the succession is to be continued by a bishop who derives his orders from an Old Catholic at one or more removes, it will be necessary to provide similar evidence for every link in the chain. As in many cases several generations of ordination are involved, such documentary evidence will be difficult, if not impossible to supply. It will scarcely be possible to prove that all of the bishops concerned, some of whom of course are from an evangelical rather than a catholic tradition within Anglicanism, shared the "profoundly catholic theology" which was one of the decisive factors in Dr. Leonard's case.

Criteria of validity

There is another significant aspect of Dr. Leonard's ordination: the fact that in his case conditional ordination was said to be appropriate because (in Fr. Jackson's words but my italics) "a doubt exists concerning the *invalidity* of his Anglican ordination." This statement inverts the logic of canon 845.2, which prescribes that a new rite of ordination is to be performed conditionally only if there is prudent doubt whether the sacrament has been already *validly* received. The burden of proof has thus been transferred: the requirement of doubt about validity is changed to doubt about invalidity. According to the canon, if there is not prudent doubt, the orders should be regarded as valid; in the Vatican's judgment absence of prudent doubt

---

[9]   Since then two former Anglican priests have been said to have received conditional ordination with the permission of Rome, but the full facts have not been made public.

creates the need for absolute ordination. In any event the arguments against the certain insufficiency of form and intention in Anglican ordinations today are strong.[10] The Lambeth endorsement of ARCIC in 1988 provides grounds for a presumption that the ordaining bishop has not a certainly insufficient intention, even though the Vatican did not recognise that the Final Report represents Catholic faith fully and without possibility of ambiguity. As for form, *Apostolicae curae* itself implicitly admits that the wording of the 1662 Prayer Book could, in itself, bear an orthodox interpretation.[11]

A comment which Cardinal Hume was reported in the press to have made a year ago suggests a wider approach to the issue of validity. Noting that at the Low Week meeting of 1994 the bishops of England and Wales had said of Anglican clergy: "We recognise in the ministry they have exercised a call from God," the Cardinal drew the tentative conclusion that "you could possibly say that the ordination could be valid." In fact the Vatican formulated a prayer to be said at Dr. Leonard's conditional ordination, recognising that the ministry of the Anglican Communion was an instrument of grace and salvation, and adding, in accordance with *Lumen Gentium* 8, that this fruitfulness was "derived from the very fullness of grace and truth entrusted to the Catholic Church."

If Anglican priests receive a call from God within their own Communion, exercise a ministry which is instrumental of grace and salvation, and do so by virtue of power entrusted to the Catholic Church, what does it mean to say their orders are invalid? Invalidity cannot be caused by the mere fact of not being in communion with the pope, for then we would have to conclude that Orthodox orders were invalid too. Bishop Christopher Butler used to say that what was lacking was the *res et sacramentum,* the position of a bishop, priest or deacon within the Church as a sacramental reality, not simply a juridical authorization. Perhaps we should postulate degrees of validity, just as we postulate degrees of communion. If so, a Roman Catholic could say that Anglican orders may have an imperfect validity, so that some form of conditional supplementary ordination would be called for.

Conclusion

We have been considering ways in which the context of the Anglican ordinals has changed, both on the Anglican and the Roman Catholic sides,

---

[10]   I apologise for the double negative, but it is forced upon me by the terms of the Vatican decision concerning Dr. Leonard.

[11]   "Even though some words of the Anglican Ordinal as it now stands *may present the possibility of some ambiguity*, they cannot bear the same sense as they have in a Catholic rite" (n. 31). The argument seems to be that in their setting the words are necessarily insufficient, though in a different setting they could be given a sufficient meaning.

and asking whether the changes imply that the verdict of 1896 no longer applies, at least in its totality, today. Perhaps our conclusion should be that the changes make at least some aspects of that verdict no longer relevant.

It must however in conclusion be stated that not all changes have increased the likelihood of Roman recognition. The ordination of women (at the time of writing there were said to be ten women bishops in the Anglican Communion), the movement for lay presidency at the Eucharist, the weakening of Anglican insistence on the indissolubility of marriage, the spread of theological liberalism, and a lack of firmness in some aspects of moral teaching combine to make it less easy for the justifiably demanding Roman authorities to acknowledge in Anglicanism the context which would make the native character of the ordination rite acceptable. On the other side, the Vatican criteria for recognition have become clearer, perhaps also stricter. I regret to have to conclude that the "new context" in which Anglican orders should be judged is not in every respect more favourable than the setting a hundred, or even nine years ago.

The Liturgical Consequences of *Apostolicae curae* for Anglican Ordination Rites

PAUL F. BRADSHAW*

Prior to the papal condemnation of Anglican orders in 1896, Anglicans had on the whole exhibited little interest in the technical issues of sacramental theology and liturgical form raised by the long-running controversy with Roman Catholics. Since they were convinced that the Anglican Ordinal clearly intended to confer the traditional orders of bishop, priest, and deacon, and contained within it what its preface proclaimed to be essentials of ordination required by the New Testament—prayer and the imposition of hands—they were largely unconcerned about such things as the proximity to the act of laying on hands of appropriate words defining the order that was supposedly being conferred. Only a few Anglicans, mainly from the Anglo-Catholic wing, attempted to engage with Roman Catholic polemicists on their own terms.[1]

While the Anglican conviction that their orders were entirely valid remained unshaken following the publication of *Apostolicae curae,* yet there have been—perhaps not surprisingly—signs of a firm desire to make twentieth-century revisions of Anglican ordination rites impregnable against any further attacks on the same grounds. Indeed, the compilers of the ordination rites in the Church of England's Alternative Service Book 1980 were willing to admit openly that "throughout the process of drafting the shadow of *Apostolicae curae* hung over the drafters."[2] What is rather more troubling is that, apparently as a consequence of this desire, Anglican liturgical revisers seem to have willingly accepted the scholastic approach to the essentials of ordination at the very time when in other areas of liturgical and sacramental theology they have been moving in quite a different direction. As a result, not only is the theology articulated by contemporary Anglican ordination rites in some ways more medieval than patristic, but it is in tension—if not outright conflict—with that expressed by other modern Anglican liturgies, and especially by eucharistic rites.

---

* Paul F. Bradshaw is Professor of Liturgy and Director of Graduate Studies in the Department of Theology at the University of Notre Dame, and former President of the North American Academy of Liturgy.

[1] For further details, see Paul F. Bradshaw, *The Anglican Ordinal: Its History and Development from the Reformation to the Present Day* (London: SPCK, 1971), pp. 71–86, 123–43.

[2] *The Alternative Service Book 1980: A Commentary by the Liturgical Commission* (London: Church Information Office, 1980), p. 143.

The defects alleged by *Apostolicae curae* to exist in the first Anglican Ordinals of 1550 and 1552 had already been remedied in part at the 1662 revision. An explicit reference to the particular order being conferred had been inserted at that time into the formularies spoken during the imposition of hands on both priests and bishops.[3] But as a result of the historical research that the Anglican orders controversy itself had largely engendered, twentieth-century Anglican revisers began to be conscious that ancient ordination rites invariably included not just prayer in general but an ordination prayer (or prayers) in close association with the laying on of hands that seemed to ask for the bestowal of the order or of "its grace and power," as the Papal Bull had put it. Since such a prayer was lacking in the 1662 rite for the diaconate, and the prayer in the rite for the priesthood contained no petition at all for the ordinands, several revisions in different parts of the Anglican Communion during the first part of the twentieth century hastened to rectify these omissions in different ways. The unsuccessful attempt at revision in England in 1927/28 added an ordination prayer for deacons and inserted a short petition into the prayer for priests. The Episcopal Church of Scotland in 1929 left the rite for the diaconate untouched but introduced a specific petition for the Holy Spirit into the ordination prayer for bishops as well as that for priests. This was copied by the Province of South Africa in 1954. Although the Anglican Church in Canada merely added an ordination prayer for deacons in its 1959 revision, the Church of India, Pakistan, Burma, and Ceylon in 1960 inserted an explicit mention of the particular order being conferred in the ordination prayers for bishops and priests, as well as adding a similar reference in the imperative formula at the imposition of hands on deacons.[4]

This Anglican trend was encouraged by the publication by Pius XII in 1947 of the Apostolic Constitution, *Sacramentum ordinis.* It provided for the very first time an official ecclesiastical statement of what were thought to constitute the essentials of ordination in the Roman Pontifical. Not surprisingly, it maintained the traditional scholastic categories of matter and form, and so declared that "the sole matter of the sacred orders of the diaconate, presbyterate, and episcopate is the laying on of hands; likewise the sole form is the words determining the application of this matter, by which are univocally signified the sacramental effects—namely, the power of the order and the grace of the Holy Spirit—and which are accepted and used as such by the Church."[5] The document then went on to define certain petitions in the classical Roman ordination prayers as constituting this es-

---

[3] Bradshaw, *The Anglican Ordinal*, pp. 92–93.
[4] *Ibid.*, pp. 162, 166, 168–69.
[5] Latin text in *Acta Apostolicae Sedis* 40 (1948): 6.

sential form. In the case of the diaconate, the vital words were said to be: "Send upon him, we pray, O Lord, the Holy Spirit, by whom, faithfully accomplishing the work of your ministry, he may be strengthened with the gift of your sevenfold grace"; for the presbyterate: "Grant, we pray, Almighty Father, the dignity of the presbyterate to this your servant; renew in his inward parts the spirit of holiness, so that he may obtain and receive from you, O God, the office of second dignity, and by the example of his behavior he may commend right conduct"; and for the episcopate: "Complete the fullness of your mystery in your priest, and equipped with all the adornments of glory, hallow him with the dew of heavenly unction."[6] It may be noted that this same approach to the essentials of ordination was also reaffirmed in the Apostolic Constitution, *Pontificalis Romani recognitio*, that accompanied the publication of the revised Roman Catholic ordination rites in 1968.[7]

The next round of Anglican revisions, therefore, went even further in the direction of introducing a similar pattern into their ordination rites, heavily influenced in this by the eminent Anglican liturgical scholar E. C. Ratcliff. He was convinced that in ancient ordination rites "the substantive clause of the Ordination Prayer was a petition asking God to send his Holy Spirit upon the person being ordained to make him a Bishop (or Priest or Deacon)."[8] The same notion—very probably derived from Ratcliff himself—can also be found in the Report of the Sub-committee on the *Book of Common Prayer* of the 1958 Lambeth Conference, which claimed that in the ordination practice of the early Church, the bishop "offered the prayer asking for the sending of the Spirit upon the candidate to make him bishop, priest, or deacon, as the case might be."[9] Since Ratcliff was a major consultant in the process of producing new ordination rites for the Church of South India, which was completed in 1958, as well as the principal architect of the proposed Ordinal for the Anglican-Methodist Unity Scheme in England, which appeared in final form in 1968, his ideas can be seen clearly reflected in those two liturgical texts. While they are both ecumenical in character rather than strictly Anglican, yet Anglican concerns about the validity of ordinations were obviously a major factor in their compilation,

---

[6]   *Ibid.*, p. 7.

[7]   Latin text in *Acta Apostolicae Sedis* 60 (1968): 369–73; English translation in *Documents on the Liturgy 1963–1979* (Collegeville: Liturgical Press, 1982), No. 324.

[8]   "A Note on Schemes of Union, the Ministry and Forms of Ordination," in David H. Tripp (ed.), *E. C. Ratcliff: Reflections on Liturgical Revision*, Grove Liturgical Study 22 (Nottingham: Grove Books, 1980), p. 30. This "Note" was a paper contributed by Ratcliff at a conference of the Theological Committee of the Church Union held on 7 January 1959 to discuss the report of the Committee on Church Unity from the 1958 Lambeth Conference.

[9]   The Lambeth Conference 1958: *The Encyclical Letter from the Bishops together with the Resolutions and Reports* (London: SPCK, 1958) 2.89.

and the two of them set the pattern that was followed in later revisions of Anglican ordination rites.

It is true that it was in fact from the ordination practice of the (Presbyterian) Church of Scotland that the Church of South India drew the original inspiration for arranging for the laying on of hands to take place during the ordination prayer itself, instead of attaching it to a short imperative formula following the prayer (which had been the Anglican custom).[10] Nevertheless, the precise form that this took betrays Ratcliff's understanding of the essentials of ordination. While in the Scottish rite the Moderator and other ministers laid their hands upon the head of the ordinand merely at the point in the prayer that the laying on of hands was mentioned, in the South Indian rite the imposition of hands was maintained throughout the central petition for the Holy Spirit: "Send down thy Holy Spirit upon thy servant N., whom we, in thy name, and in obedience to thy most blessed will, do now ordain Bishop/Presbyter/Deacon in thy Church."[11] Moreover, when more than one person was to be ordained at a time, a novel expedient was to be employed. The whole prayer was not repeated for each candidate, but instead the prayer was only recited once, and when the above sentence was reached, that alone was repeated for each ordinand while hands were laid on him. The congregation replied "Amen" each time the petition was said, and when all candidates had received the imposition of hands, the prayer was continued to its conclusion. This arrangement reveals clearly the presumption that ordination was effected by the recitation of this particular formula.

Not surprisingly, the 1968 Anglican-Methodist rites are similar. The same arrangement was adopted for the laying on of hands; the same provision was made for multiple candidates; and the petition itself in each rite closely resembled the South Indian version, differing mainly in the omission to the reference to the Church ordaining: "Send down thy Holy Spirit upon thy servant N. for the office and work of a Deacon in thy Church/for the office and work of a Presbyter in thy Church/for the office of a Bishop and Chief Pastor in thy Church."[12] In the case of the episcopate, this petition was to be said by all the bishops together—a feature previously unknown in the

---

[10]　T. S. Garrett, *Worship in the Church of South India*, 2nd ed. (London: Lutterworth Press, 1965), p. 78. See Church of Scotland, *Ordinal and Service Book for use in the Courts of the Church* (1931).

[11]　Church of South India, The Ordinal (1958); 2nd ed. in *Church of South India, Book of Common Worship* (Oxford: Oxford University Press, 1962), pp. 159–79.

[12]　*Anglican-Methodist Unity: Report of the Anglican-Methodist Unity Commission*, Part I, "The Ordinal" (London: SPCK/Epworth Press, 1968), pp. 19, 26, 32. An earlier draft had included a reference to God's calling of the candidate: "Send down thy Holy Spirit upon thy servant N., whom thou hast called to serve thee as a Deacon in thy Church"/"Send thy Holy Spirit upon thy servant N., whom thou hast called to serve thee as a Presbyter in thy Church"/ "Pour forth thy Holy Spirit upon thy servant N., whom thou hast chosen to be a Bishop and Chief Pastor in thy Church." See *Towards Reconciliation: The Interim Statement of the Anglican-Methodist Unity Commission* (London: SPCK/Epworth Press, 1967), pp. 60, 67, 72.

Anglican tradition and very probably a sign of the influence of the 1944 Apostolic Constitution *Episcopalis consecrationis* of Pope Pius XII, which put an end to centuries of debate in the Roman Catholic Church by declaring that bishops who participated in the ordination of a bishop were themselves co-consecrators and not merely assistants to the presiding bishop.[13]

Virtually all Anglican ordination rites composed since then have followed the lead given by these two Ordinals in placing the imposition of hands during the ordination prayer and in making provision for its central petition alone to be repeated when there is more than one person to be ordained. The sole exception to this rule is the Church of the Province of South Africa, which in its 1988 rite has retained the imposition of hands, with its own formula, after the ordination prayer, even when there is only one ordinand.[14]

Ancient Ordination Rites

Ratcliff's assertion concerning ancient ordination rites, cited earlier, that "the substantive clause of the Ordination Prayer was a petition asking God to send his Holy Spirit upon the person being ordained to make him a Bishop (or Priest or Deacon)" will not really stand up to close scrutiny.

In the first place, the whole idea that ancient ordination prayers had a "substantive clause" or specific central petition is anachronistic. That way of thinking is a product of medieval sacramental theology in its attempts to define the essential elements of a rite over against its more peripheral features, which was perpetuated in the Anglican orders debate. Ancient ordination prayers were not built around a single petition that encapsulated what was being sought, but usually included a variety of requests, with no one of them being thought of as less, or more, important than another. Consider, for example, the petitions in the first of the two Byzantine prayers for a deacon:

Lord, keep this man also, whom you are pleased should be appointed through me to the ministry of the diaconate, in all holiness, holding the mystery of the faith in a pure conscience. Give him the grace which you gave to Stephen your protomartyr, whom you also called first to the work of your diaconate. And make him worthy according to your good pleasure to administer the rank given to him by your goodness—for those serving well gain for themselves a good rank—and make your servant perfect. . . . [15]

---

[13]   Latin text in *Acta Apostolicae Sedis* 37 (1945): 131–32. Among subsequent Anglican rites, only the Episcopal Church in the USA has adopted this practice.

[14]   For a collection of texts of rites, see Colin Buchanan (ed.), *Modern Anglican Ordination Rites*, Alcuin/GROW Liturgical Study 3 (Nottingham: Grove Books, 1987).

[15]   Paul F. Bradshaw, *Ordination Rites of the Ancient Churches of East and West* (New York: Pueblo, 1990), p. 136.

For another example, from a quite different background, consider the petitions in the classical Gallican ordination prayer for a presbyter:

spread forth the hand of your blessing on this your servant N., whom we set apart with the honor of the presbyterate, so that he may show himself to be an elder by the dignity of his acts and the righteousness of his life, taught by these instructions which Paul presented to Titus and Timothy: that meditating on your law day and night, O almighty one, what he reads he may believe, what he believes he may teach, what he teaches he may practice. May he show in himself justice, loyalty, mercy, bravery; may he provide the example, may he demonstrate the exhortation, in order that he may keep the gift of your ministry pure and untainted; and with the consent of your people may he transform the body and blood of your Son by an untainted benediction; and in unbroken love may he reach to a perfect man, to the measure of the stature of the fullness of Christ, in the day of the justice of eternal judgment with a pure conscience, with full faith, full of the Holy Spirit. . . . [16]

Secondly, not all ancient prayers mention the gift of the Holy Spirit. Many of them certainly do, but some have no such explicit reference at all. For instance, neither of the two prayers that I have just quoted specifically asks for the bestowal of the Holy Spirit upon the ordinand. Even the classical Roman ordination prayers for bishops and presbyters contain only very incidental allusions to the third person of the Trinity. As we have seen, that for bishops actually asks God to "hallow them with the dew of heavenly unction," and it is only some lines later that it specifies that the purpose of this is "so that the power of your Spirit may both fill them within and surround them without." The prayer for presbyters is still more reticent in its language. It merely asks God to "renew in their inward parts the spirit of holiness."[17] This is not to suggest that ordination prayers ought not to ask for the gift of the Holy Spirit. After all, many of these prayers probably took their initial shape prior to the pneumatological debates in the second half of the fourth century, and so were not subject to the sort of pressures for doctrinal orthodoxy that affected later compositions. But it is to suggest that a petition for the gift of the Holy Spirit cannot be regarded as of the essence of the prayer.

Thirdly, most ancient ordination prayers do not ask that the person be made a bishop, priest, or deacon. On the contrary, the majority of rites presuppose that God has called the person to that ministry, that the person has already been made bishop, priest, or deacon through the process of election just completed, and that what is now happening in the prayer is that God is being asked to endue the new minister with the gifts and qualities requisite for the effective discharge of the office. So, for example, the ordination prayer for a presbyter in the fourth-century Apostolic Constitu-

---

[16]   *Ibid.*, p. 227.
[17]   *Ibid.*, pp. 216, 218.

tions asks God to "look now also upon this your servant who has been admitted into the presbytery by the vote and judgment of the whole clergy, and fill him with the spirit of grace and counsel to help and govern your people with a pure heart. . . . "[18] Similarly, the first of the two Byzantine prayers for a bishop asks God to "strengthen by the advent, power, and grace of your Holy Spirit him who has been elected to undertake the gospel and the high-priestly dignity . . . "; while the second, which is in its present form addressed to Christ, asks him to "make him who has been made dispenser of the high-priestly grace to be an imitator of you, the true shepherd. . . . "[19]

The first instance of ordination prayers asking for the bestowal of the office itself occurs in the Sacramentary of Sarapion, usually dated in the middle of the fourth century. While the prayer for a presbyter adheres to the more common pattern of simply asking for the gift of appropriate qualities, those for a deacon and a bishop ask God to "make this man" a deacon or bishop.[20] Such language, however, is not common. It is not found in any of the other extant texts of the patristic period, and it is relatively rare in the later ordination prayers for bishops, presbyters, and deacons in both East and West, although it is sometimes implied in some of the ancillary, and presumably later, formularies of certain rites. But among the most ancient versions of Eastern ordination prayers proper, it occurs explicitly only in one Armenian prayer for a presbyter, which asks God to "bestow on your servant the rank of priesthood"; in prayers found in both the East Syrian and Georgian rites, which ask God to "elect" the candidates to the office; and in the West Syrian prayer for a presbyter, which similarly asks God to "appoint" the person.[21] In the West, the sole occurrence of a petition of this kind is in the Roman prayer for presbyters, which asks God for the bestowal of "the dignity of the presbyterate" and of "the office of second dignity."[22] On the other hand, it must be admitted that a number of texts do understand the action of the laying on of hands as effecting the conferral of the office.

Thus, Ratcliff's definition of the essentials of ordination turns out to be less true of Christian antiquity than it is of later centuries, when the role of the Holy Spirit was more clearly defined, when the ritual action of the laying on of hands with prayer came to be thought of as the sacramental means by which the particular order was bestowed and as an authoritative commissioning rather than humble petition for the gifts needed for the exercise of an office already conferred, and when it was thought that ordination was

---

[18] *Ibid.*, p. 115.
[19] *Ibid.*, pp. 133–34.
[20] *Ibid.*, pp. 122–23.
[21] *Ibid.*, pp. 131, 159, 161, 164, 170–72, 181.
[22] *Ibid.*, p. 218.

effected at a particular moment in the rite rather than through the totality of the process.

Ordination and the Eucharist

Not only do modern Anglican ordination rites conform more closely to medieval and post-medieval ideas about the essentials of ordination than they do to ancient ones, but the sacramental theology that they reflect is very different in character from that which we see currently emerging in Anglican circles in relation to the Eucharist. There we can observe a tendency to move away from the scholastic concept of a specific "moment" of consecration within the eucharistic prayer towards the idea that the whole of the prayer should be seen as consecratory.

Although this is not an entirely new idea to Anglicanism—something similar can, for instance, be found in the writings of Herbert Thorndike in the seventeenth century[23]—yet it received its first official encouragement in the Report of the Sub-committee on the Book of Common Prayer of the 1958 Lambeth Conference. Acknowledging its indebtedness to Louis Bouyer's book, *Life and Liturgy*, the Report said that it desired "to draw attention to a conception of consecration which is scriptural and primitive and goes behind subsequent controversies with respect to the moment and formula of consecration. This is associated with the Jewish origin and meaning of *eucharistia* and may be called consecration through thanksgiving."[24] Since then, this idea has gained considerable ground throughout the Anglican Communion. We may take as an example the Church of England's draft Series 3 eucharistic rite, which appeared in 1971. Not only did it omit any rubrics concerning "manual acts" to be performed in connection with the narrative of institution, but the Liturgical Commission's official commentary on the text asserted:

It is the whole prayer which sets apart the bread and wine for their unique sacramental use. If "consecration" is the appropriate term for this setting apart—and it is a term which is not without its difficulties—then it is the offering of the whole thanksgiving over the elements within the context of the other actions of the fourfold sequence which "consecrates". If the thirteenth or the seventeenth centuries saw fit to have "moments" of consecration at the recitation of the dominical words within the narrative of institution, we cannot now be bound by those precedents.[25]

---

[23]   Herbert Thorndike, *An Epilogue to the Tragedy of the Church of England* (1659) III.4.1-25, in *The Theological Works of Herbert Thorndike* IV (Oxford: Parker, 1852), pp. 50–68.
[24]   The Lambeth Conference: 1958, 2.85.
[25]   Church of England Liturgical Commission, *A Commentary on Holy Communion:* Series 3 (London: SPCK, 1971), p. 23.

Similarly, in his survey of new eucharistic rites that had been drawn up in the Anglican Communion between 1968 and 1975, Colin Buchanan reported that:

> There has been a further move away from a "moment of consecration." Manual Acts during the narrative of institution are now a comparative rarity, the two most obvious remaining instances being the American rites and [the Irish Experimental Liturgy, 1972]. . . . It thus becomes even easier to see the whole prayer as consecratory.[26]

In the light of this trend in eucharistic practice and theology, the retention of a "moment of ordination" and of the idea of "consecration by formula" in modern Anglican ordination rites becomes even more anomalous, and can only really be explained as a consequence of the long shadow cast by *Apostolicae curae*. If these rites wanted to be consistent with what is currently happening with regard to the Eucharist and also with more primitive ordination practice and theology, they would need to treat the ordination prayer as a unity, and not break it up into what are in effect three prayers: an introductory act of praise; an essential central invocation of the Holy Spirit; and a series of less important final petitions. Likewise, the custom found in some service-books of printing the central invocation in capital letters or otherwise setting it off from the rest of the text should be discouraged.

Of course, this would still leave the problem of what to do when there was more than one candidate to be ordained at the same time. Fortunately, in many parts of the world this now occurs less frequently than it used to do because of the decrease in the number of ordinands; and one could ask whether it might not need to happen even less often if provinces followed the lead of the early Church and as a general rule ordained candidates in the local congregation in which they were to serve rather than retaining the medieval custom of ordaining at some more central location for the convenience of the ordaining bishop. To this day, the rule in the Orthodox Churches is that not more than one person may be ordained to each order during any one service.

Even if this suggestion were to be rejected, the time has certainly come to reconsider the method introduced into Anglicanism from the Church of South India. Repeating the central petition for each ordinand can only serve to encourage the misleading conclusion that this alone is what is necessary to effect an ordination. It is in essence the equivalent of repeating "This is my body" over each individual eucharistic wafer. Other, and more theologically desirable, alternatives are possible. If there were a very small number

---

[26] Colin Buchanan, *Further Anglican Liturgies 1968–1975* (Nottingham: Grove Books, 1975), pp. 17–18. Since 1975 two other modern Anglican eucharistic rites, in Australia and Wales, have retained the requirement of manual acts within the narrative of institution.

of candidates, one could repeat the whole prayer over each one of them, or better still, have the presiding bishop move along the line of ordinands, laying hands briefly on each one in turn, while the prayer itself was said only once. This would make it clear that no particular set of words in the prayer needs to be recited over each person. And if numbers were too great for this method to be practicable, there is always the arrangement adopted in the current Roman Catholic rites themselves, where the laying on of hands on each person takes place in silence immediately before the prayer, and then the prayer is recited once over them all. Although this does force a separation between the prayer and the ritual gesture, the two remain in very close proximity to one another. The only really unfortunate aspect of the Roman Catholic rites is that this is also prescribed when there is only one person to be ordained, thus separating the imposition of hands from the prayer even when there is no need to do so.

Ordination as Process

Such alterations alone in Anglican ordination rites would not, however, completely free them from the effects of *Apostolicae curae* and its scholastic presuppositions. More still needs to be done. If we think again of recent developments in eucharistic theology in both Anglican and Roman Catholic circles, we will see that there has been a much greater change than just the trend towards treating the eucharistic prayer as a unity rather than identifying a "moment of consecration" within it. Since the work of Gregory Dix,[27] it has become usual to view the role of the prayer not in isolation but as one part of the totality of the eucharistic action, as our earlier quotation from the Church of England Liturgical Commission indicated, when it said that it was "the offering of the whole thanksgiving over the elements within the context of the other actions of the fourfold sequence which 'consecrates'."[28] Similarly, in Roman Catholic theology the full realization of the presence of Christ in the eucharistic elements now tends to be linked not just to the prayer but to the act of communion.[29] Furthermore, there is a general tendency to see Christ as being present and active in various ways throughout the whole eucharistic rite. Thus, for example, the Anglican-Roman Catholic Agreed Statement on eucharistic doctrine affirms: "It is the same Lord who through the proclaimed word invites his people to his table, who through his minister presides at that table, and who gives himself sacramentally in the body and blood of his paschal sacrifice." And it goes on to say:

---

[27] *The Shape of the Liturgy* (Westminister [London]: Dacre, 1945).

[28] Church of England Liturgical Commission, *A Commentary on Holy Communion*, p. 23.

[29] See, for example, Edward Schillebeeckx, *The Eucharist* (New York: Sheed and Ward, 1968), p. 141.

The Lord's words at the Last Supper, "Take and eat; this is my body," do not allow us to dissociate the gift of the presence and the act of sacramental eating. The elements are not mere signs; Christ's body and blood become really present and are really given. But they are really present and given in order that, receiving them, believers may be united in communion with Christ the Lord.[30]

Similarly, the Roman Catholic rite for the Christian Initiation of Adults, which has begun to be widely imitated in both Anglican and other churches, embodies a sacramental theology that treats becoming a Christian as a journey rather than something which happens at a particular moment in time. The ritual act of baptism is thus set within a broader context of a sacramental process, which begins with the first tentative inquiries of a potential believer and culminates not merely in the individual's first act of participation in eucharistic fellowship but in post-baptismal mystagogy and the full integration of the Christian into the life of the Church. And in the case of both baptism and Eucharist, great stress is also laid on the importance of the active participation of the people as well as that of the ordained minister in the celebration of the rites.

If these developments in sacramental theology and practice have any relevance at all to the question of ordination, they suggest that it is not enough simply to see the whole ordination prayer as that which makes someone a minister. Not only is it important to take account of the fact that this prayer by the presiding minister is always set within the context of the prayer of the people in all traditional rites, but ordination should be seen as a process which extends even beyond the celebration of the totality of the rite. This would be a much more authentic recovery of the theology and practice of the early Church than the mere appropriation of the episcopal ordination prayer from the so-called Apostolic Tradition of Hippolytus— which is about as far as any church has gone in the direction of learning about ordination from ancient times. As Edward Schillebeeckx has argued, what was considered essential in the understanding of ordination in early Christianity was "the church's mandate or the church's sending of the minister, not the specific form in which the calling and sending takes shape."[31] Moreover, all ancient rites acknowledge that it is really God who, in and through the church, calls and appoints a person to an office, and that the prayer with imposition of hands follows this election and usually asks for the bestowal of the qualities needed for the office already given, in a somewhat similar way to the act of prayer and blessing in a traditional marriage rite,

---

[30] Anglican-Roman Catholic International Commission, *Agreed Statement on Eucharistic Doctrine*, 7, 9.

[31] Edward Schillebeeckx, *The Church with a Human Face* (London: SCM Press, 1985), p. 139.

which follows—rather than precedes or effects—the joining of the couple in matrimony.

Thus, the vital elements of a valid ordination encompass far more than just the sufficiency of a particular ritual gesture, forms of words, and intention. They extend from God's initial call of the candidate and the testing and eventual validation of that call by the church, which then appoints the ordinand to a particular ministerial charge, through the act of prayer by the people for the gifts necessary for the fruitful exercise of that ministry, of which the ordination prayer with imposition of hands forms the conclusion, to the final recognition by the people of the newly ordained's ministerial role among them, expressed in their acceptance of his or her performance of the liturgical functions belonging to that office.

To be fair, some elements of this were recognized by the Church of South India. The preface to its ordination services not only quoted from the Church's Constitution to the effect that "in all ordinations and consecrations the true Ordainer and Consecrator is God," but it viewed the presentation of the candidates to the presiding bishop as a basic and essential element in the ordination rite, constituting "the last step in the process of choice of them by the Church." The preface to the Anglican-Methodist Ordinal also included a parallel to the second of these statements. Similarly, the first Anglican Ordinal of 1550 clearly acknowledged the importance that ought to be given to the act of prayer by the whole congregation in the rite of ordination.[32] Unfortunately, however, modern Anglican thought and practice with regard to ordination has been so strongly shaped by past debate with Roman Catholics and the verdict of *Apostolicae curae* that it has virtually ignored these pointers and focused almost exclusively upon the narrow context of the disputed areas. After one hundred years, the time has surely come to break out of these constraints and set such matters within the broader framework in which they rightly belong.

---

[32] See Bradshaw, *The Anglican Ordinal,* pp. 25–29.

Anglican Orders: An Ecumenical Context

CHRISTOPHER HILL*

Last year's series of Lenten lectures given at St. James's Piccadilly in London, co-sponsored by *The Tablet*, reminded us once again that the theological issues connected with Anglican orders are inextricably bound up with the ancient rivalry of two opposing religious communities. As Peter Cornwell (the former Vicar of St. Mary the Virgin, Oxford, now a Roman Catholic priest) said in one of these lectures, "The Roman judgement can be seen as the climax of a process in which two religious communities sought to distance themselves from each other."[1]

Any way forward will need to take into account the fact that both the Anglican and Roman Catholic communities in England have established their identities over-and-against each other. Recognition of this can be cathartic and the setting of our rival identities in a wider ecumenical context will be a necessary step towards the reconciliation of our Churches, and thus of our ministries. In this paper I shall suggest something of this wider ecumenical context. But first a preliminary Anglican observation which at first sight will sound like the antithesis of an ecumenical approach.

It has to be said and repeated that Anglicans, by and large, do not have a problem about their orders. That is to say Anglican clergy and lay people throughout the world go to the Eucharist, to ordinations, to confirmations *without* an agony of doubt as to whether they are participating in real sacraments, or some charade. Even the clergy who have recently in England come into full communion with the Roman Catholic Church because of the ordination of women to the priesthood do not generally give doubts about their orders as their reason for a change in allegiance. The former Bishop of London clearly did not doubt his Anglican ministry—whatever we think of the reasoning behind his exceptional ordination *sub-conditione*, about which I shall say more later. Nor did Peter Cornwell, to quote from his St. James's Piccadilly lecture, which he significantly entitled "Real Priests?": "At my last (Anglican) Eucharist in the university church of St Mary in Oxford I still had no doubts. My uncertainties had to do, not with ministry, but with the centre of Catholic unity." The *problem*, Anglicans would say, is in *Apostolicae curae*

---

* Christopher Hill is Canon Residentiary and Precentor of St. Paul's Cathedral in London. He has been a member of the first and second Anglican-Roman Catholic International Commissions. Christopher Hill has been nominated Bishop of Stafford in the Diocese of Lichfield.
[1]   "Real Priests?", *The Tablet*, 1 April 1995.

87

itself and the perceived precedent of past practice it was based upon, both fuelled by climactic religious rivalry.

But of course it is not as easy as that. Anglicans cannot quite dismiss the problem or we would not be at this Conference today. The reconciliation of memories and recognition of ministries is a mutual thing. The re-establishment of *communicatio in sacris* obliges us to face the problem together. Reconciliation and communion, by definition, must be mutual. Moreover, we should not discount the psychological or theological effects of *Apostolicae curae* on Anglican identity since 1896.

This is an interesting and not entirely irrelevant digression. The Anglican archbishops retained their dignity in *Saepius officio,* their reply to Pope Leo; but only just. They rightly discerned that *Apostolicae curae* was aimed at overthrowing the whole position of the Church of England as a Church. Bishop Bell of Chichester, usually the model of an eirenic ecumenist, once called the Bull "one of the sharpest and most public rebuffs that the Church of Rome can ever have administered."[2]

An unnoticed consequence of this "rebuff" was the collapsing of the Anglican ecumenical agenda into the narrow question of orders and succession. From 1908 to 1911 the major question before the Anglican-Swedish Conversations from the Anglican side was the question of the Swedish episcopal succession. This was not a Swedish preoccupation. The Anglican Report of 1911, presented to the Lambeth Conference of 1920, was largely concerned with the unbroken succession in Sweden and a right conception of the episcopal office.

Equally, Anglican conversations with the Old Catholics were dominated by the question of apostolic succession narrowly conceived in terms of the historical episcopal succession. Though the Bonn Agreement of 1931 does not speak explicitly of Anglican orders, this is because the Old Catholic Churches of the Union of Utrecht had *already* recognised Anglican orders in 1925, after a series of conversations upon the subject. The Protocols which were drawn up for signature by Anglican and Old Catholic bishops sharing in each others' episcopal ordinations after 1931 are impossible to understand without the background of *Apostolicae curae.* These Latin Protocols are formidable documents and make absolutely explicit the intention of both Anglican and Old Catholic co-consecrators. The visiting bishops are genuine co-ministers, not merely witnesses or assistants. What is being conferred is said to be "episcopal order according to the mind of the Catholic and Apostolic Church . . . [with] . . . the fullness of all sacerdotal functions as understood in the Catholic Church everywhere, always and by all". Two *existing* streams of succession from the Apostles are acknowledged as having joined. One has to ask why such documents were drawn up for

---

[2] *Christian Unity: the Anglican Position* (London: Hodder and Stoughton, 1948).

signature at each shared episcopal ordination. And who was doing the doubting? The only answer is the spectre of Leo XIII.

More surprising is the fact that even the Orthodox were drawn into the Anglican preoccupation with orders. Although the predominant Orthodox ecclesiology would never separate a discussion of ministry from church, the Anglican-Orthodox discussions from 1920 onwards constantly returned to questions of orders and inter-communion.[3] In 1922 the Ecumenical Patriarch and Holy Synod of Constantinople were persuaded to speak of Anglican orders. They did so in Delphic terms by declaring that Anglican orders possessed "the same validity as the Roman, Old Catholic and Armenian Churches possess". At least some Orthodox theologians would have doubted that these Churches were real Churches and that they therefore lacked an authentic ministry!

Jerusalem and Cyprus followed in 1923 by provisionally acceding that Anglican priests should not be re-ordained if they became Orthodox. Romania endorsed Anglican Orders in 1936. Greece was not so sure, arguing that the whole of Orthodoxy must come to a decision, but it spoke of Anglican orders in the same somewhat detached un-Orthodox language.

Therefore, one major and unnoticed consequence of *Apostolicae curae*, I would argue, has been that the Bull subconsciously so dented Anglican self-esteem that it *distorted* Anglican ecumenical approaches to other churches. Since 1896 we have over-emphasized the issue of episcopal succession as an unconscious compensation for *Apostolicae curae.*

The discussion in England and elsewhere about the proposals contained in *The Porvoo Common Statement* between the British and Irish Anglican Churches and the Nordic and Baltic Lutheran Churches illustrates a continuing anxiety. Almost all the opposition to *The Porvoo Common Statement* has focused on the complicated story of the episcopal succession at and after the Reformation in Denmark to the virtual exclusion of other theological issues and the other countries and churches involved. Because a discussion of the Danish episcopal succession lifts us immediately out of the historical, communal and theological impasse of the English Anglican-Roman Catholic debate, it may be helpful to look at the Danish "problem" as part of an exercise in trying to set the question of Anglican Orders in a wider ecumenical context. We thus move from the past effects of *Apostolicae curae* to a way forward.

Two perspectives are adopted in the *Porvoo Common Statement:* historical and ecclesiological. The historical perspective has entailed the examination of what actually happened in Denmark in the 16th century. Lutheran and Roman Catholic historians still have different emphases: Lutherans stress the decay of the Church at the eve of the Reformation and

[3]   cf. V.T. Istavridis, *Orthodoxy and Anglicanism* (London: SPCK, 1966).

the fact that four out of the seven Danish sees were occupied by persons who had not received consecration to episcopal orders on the eve of the Reformation, though exercising jurisdiction and receiving the temporalities of the sees some were laymen. Thus on this view the Reformation was generally welcomed. Catholic historians, however, stress that there were at least two outstanding episcopal figures in the Danish Church and that the Reformation was resisted.[4] There are similarities between this debate and the lively current discussion in England about the strength of popular Catholic piety on the eve of the Reformation.[5]

The Porvoo Common Statement makes much of the actual historical continuities on the ground in the Nordic countries. The ancient sees were retained with their continuing pattern of a pastoral ministry of Word and Sacrament. There was change but in the context of a recognizable continuity of sacramental worship and pastoral care.

The complimentary theological perspective involved a comparative study of the ordination rites of all the Churches. It was found in all the Churches that the ordination or consecration of a bishop takes place in a eucharistic context, usually in the cathedral of the diocese, and is conducted by the archbishop or presiding bishop of the province assisted by the other bishops. The candidate is presented to the people and declared elected. Scriptures are read about commissioning, service, bishops, shepherding, priesthood, preaching and guiding. The candidate is interrogated as to apostolic faith and morals and the role of a bishop. The *Veni Creator* is sung and the laying on of hands follows with prayer asking the grace of God for the candidate to do the work of a bishop, and affirming that this pastoral ministry is understood to be associated with the apostles. Episcopal insignia are also given.

While the historical argument is not alone decisive this theological/liturgical evidence is persuasive. As well as an examination of the ordination

---

[4]   cf. Georg Schwaiger, *Die Reformation in den nordischen Ländern* (Munich, 1962), and the essay on Denmark in *Together in Mission and Ministry*, by Gerhard Pedersen, *The Porvoo Common Statement with Essays on Church and Ministry in Northern Europe* (London: Church House Publishing, 1993).

[5]   This debate is associated with revisionist English Reformation historians such as Eamon Duffey, Jack Scarisbrick, Richard Rex, and Christopher Haigh. Eamon Duffey has popularised this approach through his weighty and sensitive book *The Stripping of the Altars*, recently summarised in the first of the St James's Piccadilly Lectures to which I have already referred. The revisionist history in England has stressed local conservatism in religious conviction and discontinuity at the Reformation. Other historical studies, however, underline the *continuity* in the parishes and in church administration. For example, a recent study by Professor R. H. Helmholz shows the general continuity of personnel in the Church courts at national and diocesan levels in England throughout the reigns of Henry, Edward, Mary and Elizabeth. In spite of the restraint of appeals to Rome, the daily life of the Church courts, then affecting the laity very considerably in relation to moral offences, oaths, marriage disputes, the care of children, and testamentary matters, remained fundamentally the same; *Ecclesiastical Law Journal*, Volume 3, July 1995.

rites *The Porvoo Common Statement* also offers an important and fresh understanding of apostolic succession as pertaining to the *whole* church— clergy and laity as well as bishops. On this view, the historic episcopate is seen as the sacramental *sign* of the apostolic succession of the whole Church. This is of course the language of *Baptism, Eucharist and Ministry*[6] and behind it lies the earlier work of the French Catholic-Protestant Groupe des Dombes.[7]

The argument in the *Porvoo Common Statement* shows how it is possible to move away from the vexed question of episcopal "pedigree" which has dominated the discussion of Anglican orders for a century. There are of course important differences between the Danish and English Reformation episcopal successions. Nevertheless the English Recusants did not have a high opinion of the credentials of the Edwardine "State Bishops." An ecumenical comparison is therefore instructive and points to a fresh examination of the episcopal ordinations themselves and the intention of an ecclesial community in performing an episcopal ordination.

In making a fresh examination of the meaning of ordination it may be helpful to move outside a purely Western Christian framework. Metropolitan John Zizioulas of Pergamon has made an important Orthodox contribution to the understanding of apostolic continuity and succession.[8] John Zizioulas notes that the Church has traditionally approached apostolic continuity in two ways: one historical; the other eschatological. He cites I Clement as expressing a historical model in which God sends Christ and Christ sends the Apostles as the basis of apostolic succession. In Ignatius of Antioch, however, Zizioulas detects another model in which the imagery is not so much a "sending" as a "gathering" of the apostles around the Lord. The spirit "convokes" the Church around the eucharistic table.

Continuity here is guaranteed and expressed not by way of succession from generation to generation and from individual to individual, but in and through the convocation of the Church in one place, i.e. through its *eucharistic structure*. It is a *continuity of communities* and *Churches* that constitutes and expresses apostolic succession in this approach.

Zizioulas does not of course argue for the abandonment of the "historical approach." He argues for a synthesis of the two approaches. But the synthesis is a radical one and has important ecumenical implications. He speaks of "a pneumatological conditioning of history by eschatology" and an *epicletic* aspect of continuity.

---

[6]   Faith and Order Paper No. 111, Geneva: World Council of Churches, 1982.
[7]   To be found in *Modern Ecumenical Documents on the Ministry* (London: SPCK, 1975).
[8]   "Apostolic Continuity and Succession," in *Being as Communion*, (London: DLT, 1985).

In an epicletical context history ceases to be in itself a guarantee of security. The *epiclesis* means ecclesiologically that the Church *ask to receive from God what she has already received historically from Christ as if she had not received it at all*, i.e. as if history did not count in itself.

So Zizioulas argues that "there is no security to be found in any historical guarantee as such—be it ministry or word or sacrament or even the historical Christ Himself."

He further argues that one of the greatest misfortunes for the Church came when ordination came to be regarded as being concerned with "history" rather than "eschatology." Ordination must be seen in the eschatological, gathered, convoked, context of the whole Church. The historical approach alone, he continues, leads to a limiting of apostolic continuity to the ordained ministry, whereas the eschatological approach leads to the conclusion that the baptized laity are as essential to ordination as clergy. The Church relates to the apostles not only through ordination but also through baptism. Episcopal succession is essentially an expression of the visibility of the *succession of communities.* So Zizioulas rejects a notion of apostolic "linear history"—the problems of which he notes are still with us in the ecumenical dialogues. Not least, I would add, in the question of Anglican Orders. Unfamiliar as Zizioulas's language may sometimes be his general argument is clear enough and important for all Orthodox, Catholic and Protestant dialogues on ministry.

In such a perspective we must look at the presence of the Church gathered by the Spirit in the eucharistic assembly with the intention of commissioning a bishop to pastor the local flock. Gathered by the Spirit and invoking the Spirit, the *whole* of this assembly have their parts to play: historical continuity does not become the be all and end all of ordination—as it is for "Episcopi Vagantes" sects who may, arguably, have the "sign" of apostolic succession but certainly not its reality. The authenticity of an ordination depends upon the spirit in the whole Church, not upon a particular history of ministerial succession.

Such a view is ecumenically liberating, provided a church is already able to recognise the "ecclesiality" of another church. John Zizioulas is not alone in wanting to begin with the Church rather than the ordained ministry. Roman Catholic sacramental theologians, ecclesiologists and ecumenists have for many years stressed the ecclesiological dimension of the ecumenical quest. But Vatican II, perhaps unhappily, drew a distinction between the Eastern Churches and the Western Churches which experienced the Reformation. And the difference between the Eastern and Western separated churches was focused on the possession of a valid ministry and eucharist. We are thus locked into a circular argument. George Tavard well sums up this problematic towards the end of his valuable *Review of Anglican*

Orders.[9] The necessity for the prior recognition of ministry and eucharist locks us back into the historical debate; unless we take seriously the *Porvoo* approach to continuity and ecclesial intention and hear Zizioulas's plea for a new synthesis to redress the balance between the eschatological notion of the Church and an over-historicized Western Christianity.

With this wider horizon Anglicans can look again at *Apostolicae curae* itself. As Anglicans approach its centenary we can say a number of good things about it whatever the motives of those who drafted it. It officially disposed of the Nag's Head fable. It understands episcopacy in terms of a distinct order of ministry—not as the medieval church often did, merely as an office of heightened jurisdiction. And it also, importantly, focused attention on the issue of "sacramental intention." In all these things I believe the Bull was right. As an Anglican I do not accept the conclusions it actually draws from its argument about "intention" which apparently relies on the disputable opinion that an alleged intention *not* to ordain a "sacrificing priesthood" automatically cancels out an obvious and clearly stated intention to do what the Church does, namely to continue the Apostolic ministry of bishops, priests and deacons, as explicitly stated in the Preface to the Ordinal. The other serious problem about intention in the Bull is its total silence about the Preface. To ignore the Preface to the Ordinal when trying to discern its intention was a curious, serious and fatal error: a point rightly emphasised in the *Responsio* of the Anglican archbishops.

It was to deal with the problem of intention that ARCIC-I formulated its Agreed Statements on *Eucharistic Doctrine* and *Ministry and Ordination,* with their *Elucidations.* Ten years ago, Cardinal Willebrands spoke of a new possibility, a new context, in which the Anglican Communion would be able to state formally that it professes the same faith as the Catholic Church on these matters, and thus "the Ordinal might no longer retain that *nativa indoles* which was the basis for Pope Leo's judgement." Since then there has been the Lambeth Conference Resolution on the *Final Report* of ARCIC, the Vatican *Response, Clarifications* and Cardinal Cassidy's official assurance that: "the Agreement reached on Eucharist and Ministry by ARCIC-I is thus greatly strengthened and no further study would seem to be required at this stage."[10] This sounds to be ultimately hopeful, though it obviously prescinds from the debate about women's ordination and would be jeopardized if an Anglican Province decided to authorise the celebration of the eucharist by lay persons, other than by the traditional way of the laying on of hands with prayer by a bishop. But there are also further complications: if only on the side-lines of the Great Debate.

The decision by Rome to ordain *sub conditione* certain former Anglican

9   Pages 114ff (Collegeville, Minnesota: The Liturgical Press, 1990).
10   For all the above see, *Anglicans and Roman Catholics: The Search for Unity,* eds. C.J. Hill and E.J. Yarnold (London: SPCK/CTS), 1994.

clergy seems moderately helpful. Any crack in the practice of absolute ordinations is a step in the right direction. But the grounds for the decision—at least as reported—seem curious. One would have expected the grounds to have been based solely on the Old Catholic co-consecrations already referred to. But the *personal* intentions of the candidate seem to have been equally decisive, reported reference being made to a diary kept at the time of ordination. But the work of ARCIC-I, the decisions of the Lambeth Conference, General Synods and the Pontifical Council for Christian Unity have all assumed that the sacramental intention to which attention must be paid is that of the *official* Church, as found in its liturgies, and theological statements.

The debate among theologians between a "personal" and "external" or "objective" sacramental intention is a long one. One interpretation of *Apostolicae curae* would certainly maintain that the personal intentions of the English Reformers cancelled any general intention to do what the Church does in ordination. But the whole direction of ARCIC and contemporary sacramental theology has surely been towards a more corporate, official, interpretation of intention. Until the Graham Leonard case this was unchallenged. A corporate view of sacramental intention would suggest that all those Anglicans who have been ordained in recent years by a bishop in whom "the twin streams of succession," Anglican and Old Catholic, have merged, would be qualified for conditional ordination. To go down a more personal route would be fraught with uncertainty. Such an approach has always involved the danger of ultimate uncertainty about *any* sacramental action.

Once again the approach suggested by John Zizioulas is helpful. If it is the *whole* Church gathered together by the Spirit which is important, we are thus released from the tyranny of individual private opinion. On such a view sacramental intention must be the explicit *public* intention of the liturgy authorized by the whole Church and *the fact itself* of the gathering of the people of God of a given place to celebrate the eucharist and to invoke the Holy Spirit to manifest the *present* apostolic continuity of the Church through the sign of the laying on of hands by a bishop. Once again a wider ecumenical context offers a positive frame of reference for an ultimate solution to the problem.

In the period immediately preceeding *Apostolicae curae* Lord Halifax and the Abbé Portal were right to hope and work for a way forward on Anglican orders. But they were wrong to suppose that this can be done irrespective of the wider reconciliation of the separated ecclesial communities of which the non-recognition of ministries is characteristically a symptom rather than a cause. At the present time of ecumenical uncertainty, we ought to be profoundly thankful that the Anglican and Roman Catholic Churches are *irreversibly* well along the road towards such ecclesial reconciliation, whatever road-blocks may currently exist. A wider ecumenical context may now offer us hope for the future. And one hundred years on we can still be encouraged and inspired by the words of Halifax to Portal in response to the latter's letter on the publication of the Bull:

We tried to do something which I believe God inspired. We have failed, for the moment; but if God wills it, His desire will be accomplished, and if He allows us to be shattered, it may well be because He means to do it Himself. This is no dream. The thing is as certain as ever.

Developments since then prove Halifax and Portal right in their vision but wrong in their estimation of the time-scale. Perhaps the same is also true for those who worked in and with the first Anglican-Roman Catholic International Commission. But the vision is still sure, even if the goal is an uncertain distance off.

The Ordination of Women: A New Obstacle to the Recognition of Anglican Orders

SARA BUTLER*

Introduction

Pope John Paul II's apostolic letter on priestly ordination, *Ordinatio sacerdotalis*,[1] took many by surprise. Its fundamental judgment has been consistently and firmly advanced in the context of the Anglican-Roman Catholic dialogue for some twenty years; still, many who wait for the full communion of Anglicans and Roman Catholics viewed it as a preemptory judgment, the closing of the door on an issue barely raised. Anglicans who have concluded that no theological objections prohibit and some positive theological arguments support, and even require the admission of women to priesthood and episcopate expressed dismay, as if betrayed. Some said the pope was responsible for erecting a "new, grave obstacle" to the restoration of communion.

Anglicans, after almost fifty years of debate,[2] decided at Lambeth in 1968 that arguments for and against the ordination of women to the priesthood were inconclusive—leaving the member churches free to act as they saw fit. But in 1968, Roman Catholics had barely begun to discuss the issue.[3] Since vigorous debate over 25–30 years has not given rise to a solid consensus among theologians, many Roman Catholics also regarded the papal letter as bringing premature closure to a relatively new question.

Nevertheless, the actual admission of Anglican women to the priesthood, and in some provinces to the episcopate, has required, for the sake of frank and sincere dialogue, some judgment from the Roman Catholic Church. And the judgment has been that it is the canonical change in *Anglican* practice which poses—in words first used by Pope Paul VI in 1976—a "new" and "grave obstacle," even a "threat,"[4] to the reconciliation of ministries. As a consequence of its ecumenical commitments, the Vatican

---

* Sara Butler, M.S.B.T., is a member of the faculty of theology at the University of St. Mary of the Lake, Mundelein, Illinois. She is a member of the second Anglican-Roman Catholic International Commission.

[1] "Apostolic Letter on Ordination and Women," *Origins* 24 (June 9, 1994), 49, 51–52.

[2] See Jacqueline Field-Bibb, *Women Towards Priesthood: Ministerial Politics and Feminist Praxis* (Cambridge: Cambridge University Press, 1991), 67–175.

[3] For the beginnings of this debate, see the Translator's Foreword, by Arlene and Leonard Swidler, to Haye van der Meer's, *Women Priests in the Catholic Church?: A Theological-Historical Investigation* (Philadelphia: Temple University Press, 1973), ix–xxix.

[4] "Letters Exchanged by Pope & Anglican Leader," *Origins* 6 (August 12, 1976), 129, 131–32, at 132.

has developed an evaluation, given its judgment, and now, in this apostolic letter, required that it be definitively held.

Different timetables, different procedures for coming to a decision, different ways of exercising teaching authority, then, have led us to this point: just as the prospect of removing the "old" obstacle to Roman Catholic recognition of Anglican orders is in sight,[5] a "new" obstacle has taken its place.

How might we get some purchase on this question? What can we learn from what has already been worked out? What is the state of the question on this topic as it has emerged from official, public Anglican-Roman Catholic documentation and exchange?[6]

I intend to review four phases of our common history with this topic, drawing upon the pertinent documentation, including reports of the Anglican-Roman Catholic Consultation in the U.S. (ARC-USA) that directly addressed the ordination of women. In the course of this review, I will call attention to two different avenues of approach. Then I will propose that *Ordinatio sacerdotalis* specifies the characteristic Roman Catholic approach, and point out what this suggests as the focus of our future efforts to address this issue.

Four Phases in the Emerging Anglican-Roman Catholic Dialogue

A. The First Phase: 1968–75

In the summer of 1968, the Malta Report was endorsed first by Cardinal Bea and a few weeks later by the Lambeth Conference. During that same Lambeth meeting, Anglican bishops adopted a resolution finding the theological arguments both for and against the ordination of women to the priesthood inconclusive.[7] Just as the Anglican-Roman Catholic International Commission (ARCIC) was being initiated, then, the Anglican Communion was nearing the conclusion of its long debate.

---

[5]   See the letter of Jan Cardinal Willebrands to the co-chairmen of ARCIC-II: "New Context for Discussing Anglican Orders," *Origins* 15 (March 20, 1986), 662–64.

[6]   I will limit my consideration to official communications, aware that this introduces a certain unreality into the report. The "Anglican position" is the position taken by Lambeth Conferences and articulated by the Archbishops of Canterbury; not all Anglicans or member churches are committed to this position. The "Roman Catholic position" is authoritatively articulated by the popes and by the responsible Vatican congregations and their spokesmen; still, many prominent Roman Catholic theologians do not find it convincing, and some explicitly propose the same arguments and conclusions as the Anglicans who favor the ordination of women.

[7]   Resolution no. 34 in *The Lambeth Conference 1968: Resolutions and Reports* (London: S.P.C.K, 1968), 39.

Reasons given in support of the 1968 resolution include the following theological considerations[8]: (1) the need to take with utmost seriousness the appeal to Sacred Scripture and Tradition; (2) the fact that "the data of Scripture appear divided on this issue"; (3) and that the data of tradition found in the early fathers and the medieval theologians reflect "biological assumptions about the nature of woman and her relation to man which are considered unacceptable" today. It concludes from the third consideration: "If the ancient and medieval assumptions about the social role and inferior status of women are no longer accepted, the appeal to tradition is virtually reduced to the observation that there happens to be no precedent for ordaining women to be priests."

As the Episcopal Church moved towards its decision to admit women to priesthood during the early 1970s, these same points were addressed: the inconclusive character of the New Testament witness, the lack of convincing evidence from early canons and ordination rites, and the obsolete view of women's inferior and subordinate status held by medieval theologians.[9] Many Anglican and Roman Catholic theologians recognized that the traditional theological arguments, based on a faulty anthropology, were indefensible.[10] They concluded, therefore, that there was no theological objection to the ordination of women.

The absence of a serious dogmatic obstacle was only the negative half of the argument; positively, they found "urgent theological reasons" in favor of the priestly ordination of women. The equality of the sexes demanded a presentation of Christian doctrine that would explicitly propose the universality of redemption, the inclusivity of the Church as a priestly body, and women's capacity to represent humanity, the Church, Christ, and God. As the 1976 General Convention approached, advocates in the Episcopal Church saw little on the ecumenical horizon to discourage them from the expectation that a difference in practice—it was viewed as a disciplinary, not a doctrinal matter—could be accommodated within, and might even be a prophetic sign for the one Church of Christ.[11]

Following the illegal ordinations in Philadelphia in 1974, however, Jan Cardinal Willebrands told some bishops of the Episcopal Church that the move from theory to practice would seriously affect the Anglican-Roman

---

[8]   *Ibid.*, the Committee Report, "Women and the Priesthood," 106–108, at 106.

[9]   J. Robert Wright, "Documentation and Reflection: An Address in Favor of the Ordination of Women to the Priesthood," *Anglican Theological Review* 55 (January, 1973), 68–72. A summary of the arguments in favor and documentation from the Episcopal Church may be found in Emily C. Hewitt and Suzanne R. Hiatt, *Women Priests: Yes or No?* (New York: The Seabury Press, 1973).

[10]   For an early and influential investigation of the anthropological question, see George H. Tavard, *Woman in Christian Tradition* (Notre Dame: University of Notre Dame Press, 1973). The work of Haye van der Meer, cited in n. 3 above, argued that this faulty anthropology might reveal the "tradition" to be determined by socio-cultural rather than theological factors.

[11]   Wright, "Documentation and Reflection," 70–71.

Catholic dialogue on the nature of ministry.[12] In October, 1975, Joseph Cardinal Bernardin, then president of the National Conference of Catholic Bishops, followed up with a statement reasserting the Catholic Church's teaching that women are not to be ordained to the priesthood.[13] Earlier that year, in an address to the Vatican's Study Commission on the Role of Women in Society and in the Church, Pope Paul VI had expressed, almost parenthetically, the basis for this judgment: "Although women do not receive the call to the apostolate of the Twelve and therefore to the ordained ministries, they are nonetheless invited to follow Christ as disciples and co-workers. . . . We cannot change what our Lord did, nor his call to women."[14]

The two different approaches, then, are these: the one—which I shall refer to as "Anglican"—proceeds by way of theological reasoning, and has its base in a renewed theological anthropology; the other—the "Roman Catholic"—proceeds by appeal to the will of Christ revealed in history and confirmed in the experience of the Church.

During this first, American, phase of our common experience with this question, attention focussed almost exclusively on the first approach. The arguments were scrutinized by ARC-USA since the prospect of action on the part of the Episcopal Church was imminent. The ARC-USA co-chairmen convened a special scholarly consultation in June, 1975, and its members prepared a joint statement on the relation of this question to the "authority of the Church's tradition."[15] According to their statement, the ordination of women raises "issues which cannot be answered adequately by the mere citing of traditional practices of belief," for the traditional reasons for refusing women ordination are "not universally acceptable." In addition, "problems relating to the doctrine of God, of the Incarnation and Redemption" were seen to be "at least indirectly involved in its solution." Participants agreed that "any decision, whether for or against the ordination of women, will in fact require the church to explain or develop its essential Tradition in an unprecedented way."

By 1975, the Episcopal Church had completed its theological exploration and was on the verge of making an authoritative decision. The position of the Roman Catholic Church—not yet developed as it has been in the intervening years—was not, according to the pope, expected to change, though popular opinion in favor of change was mounting, and theological investigation was beginning in earnest. The ARC-USA consultation quite

---

[12] "Women Priests and Ecumenism," *Origins* 5 (October 9, 1975), 241, 243–44, at 243.
[13] "Discouraging Unreasonable Hopes," *Origins* 5 (October 16, 1975), 257, 259–60.
[14] "Women/Disciples and Co-Workers," *Origins* 4 (May 1, 1975), 718–19, at 719.
[15] "Ordination of Women/an Ecumenical Dialogue," *Origins* 5 (July 17, 1975), 100. The papers from this consultation were later published as *Pro and Con on Ordination of Women* ((New York: Seabury Professional Services, 1976).

realistically observed that each Church would have to arrive at a decision by means of its own processes.

ARC-USA incorporated the conclusions of the special consultation into a Statement on the Ordination of Women formulated at its October, 1975 meeting.[16] In addition, it named the following common presuppositions: ARCIC's Windsor and Canterbury Statements, Scripture and Tradition as doctrinal sources, the responsibility of theologians to incorporate the findings of other sciences into their work, the fundamental equality of men and women in society and in the Church—"in exercising the ministry of all baptized persons in the public forum."[17] This Statement identified three challenges to be faced: (1) Jesus' choice of males as apostles, cited as a model, and the Church's subsequent practice was a weighty precedent whose explanation and normative character had to be newly evaluated; (2) the exclusion of a large class of persons (granted that no individual has a right to ordination) for no reason other than gender required justification by cogent arguments; and (3) a strong positive case, not just the absence of obstacles, should be proposed by those in favor of ordaining women.

In the mid 1970s, two conclusions drawn by the special consultation in the U.S. shaped the ongoing work of ARC-USA. First, all were convinced that this question was being posed in a new way and would therefore be solved only by a *development* of the tradition, a development of doctrine. Second, the required development of doctrine would involve correlating new appreciation of the equality of women and the meaning of human sexuality with the doctrines of God, the Incarnation and Redemption, and the Church and its ministry. The motivating factor was concern for the recognition of women's full equality in the world, in the economy of salvation, and in church life—what we would recognize today as the concerns of feminist theology. Since common theological objections appealed to women's state of subjection (and consequent inability to represent eminence), the first line of response was to provide theological justification for women's equality with men and their capacity to represent God, Christ and the Church. A second line of response on the part of some members of both communions was to argue, positively, that the admission of women to priesthood is required by these doctrinal developments.

In 1975, the year prior to the Minneapolis General Convention (September, 1976), the Archbishop of Canterbury, Donald Coggan, wrote to Pope Paul VI to advise him of "the slow but steady growth of a consensus of opinion within the Anglican Communion that there are no fundamental objections in principle to the ordination of women to the priesthood."[18] In

---

[16] (ARC-USA) "Christian Unity & Women's Ordination," *Origins* 5 (November 20, 1975), 349–52.

[17] *Ibid.*, no. 4, 350.

[18] "Letters Exchanged" (cited in n. 4), 129.

response, the pope advised him of the Catholic Church's conviction that "very fundamental reasons" make ordaining women to the priesthood impossible. He itemized three reasons: "the example recorded in the sacred scriptures of Christ choosing his apostles only from among men, the constant practice of the Church, which has imitated Christ in choosing only men, and [the Catholic Church's] living teaching authority which has consistently held that the exclusion of women from the priesthood is in accordance with God's plan for his church."[19] In the same letter, the pope observed that this new course of action on the part of Anglicans would inevitably introduce "an element of grave difficulty" into the dialogue between the two communions. In a second exchange of letters in early 1976, the Archbishop of Canterbury said that Anglicans saw the new development as allowing for the genuine expression of diversity in unity, but the pope responded that his affection for the Anglican Communion was the measure of the sadness he felt at the prospect of "so grave a new obstacle and threat" on the path of reconciliation.[20]

B. The Second Phase: 1976–78

A new phase in the Anglican-Roman Catholic dialogue on the issue—hardly separable from the intra-Catholic debate—began when a report of the Pontifical Biblical Commission was leaked to the press in 1976.[21] Asked to consider the question "whether or not women can be ordained to the priestly ministry (especially as ministers of the Eucharist and as leaders of the Christian community)," the Commission replied that, by itself, the New Testament did not provide a clear answer one way or the other.

Much more significant was the appearance, in January, 1976 of a *Declaration on the Question of the Admission of Women to the Ministerial Priesthood (Inter insigniores),* prepared by the Congregation for the Doctrine of the Faith and published with the approval of the pope.[22] It provided a new statement of the Roman Catholic position. A commentary released at the same time as the Declaration, but not carrying the same authority, supplies a very useful interpretation.[23]

The Declaration makes the case that there is an unbroken, universal Tradition, common to East and West, of admitting only men to ministerial

---

[19] *Ibid.,* 131.
[20] *Ibid.,* 132.
[21] "Can Women Be Priests?" *Origins* 6 (July 1, 1976), 92–96.
[22] "Vatican Declaration: Women in the Ministerial Priesthood," *Origins* 6 (February 3, 1977), 517, 519–24; *AAS* 69 (1977), 98–116.
[23] "A Commentary on the Declaration," *Origins* 6 (February 3, 1977), 524–31. The *Origins* edition lacks footnotes. Both the Declaration and the complete Commentary were published in a United States Catholic Conference pamphlet in 1977. I will cite page numbers from *Origins.*

priesthood, and that this is rooted in the example of Jesus and the apostles. It announces that the Church, "in fidelity to the Lord, does not consider herself authorized to admit women to priestly ordination."[24] This teaching, found in the first four sections of the Declaration, is proposed with the authority of the magisterium. Sections five and six, which explore the fittingness of this practice in light of the mystery of Christ and the mystery of the Church, are not.

I do not intend to repeat all the arguments of the Declaration, but I would call attention to four claims. First, the Church's universal and unbroken tradition provides the correct interpretation of the New Testament data. Second, the New Testament basis is Jesus' example in choosing the Twelve, confirmed in the practice and teaching of the apostles. Third, Jesus' choice does not reflect a cultural bias against women because there is evidence that he broke with the customs of his time in his attitude toward women. Fourth, whenever innovations were introduced, the Church has been alert to reject them immediately. The fact of a tradition traced back to Jesus and his call of the Twelve, then, is given as the essential reason. The New Testament, apart from this tradition, could not provide this certainty: it is the tradition which sees a norm in Jesus' example. Analyzing the New Testament text with contemporary methods cannot, by itself, either establish or disprove this interpretation. It is founded in the concrete evidence of history, and understood by the Church's unfolding discernment as binding.[25]

What is *not* part of the Declaration's teaching? First, it does not substantiate its view by appeal to St. Paul's injunctions (1 Cor 14:34–35 and 1 Tim. 2:12) against public teaching by women and their exercise of authority over men, nor by his teaching regarding male headship and female subordination. Second, it does not defend the faulty anthropology of St. Thomas. The Commentary notes that explanations found in medieval theologians based on the inferiority of women vis-à-vis men, and the view that women are in a "state of submission" have been abandoned.[26] The Declaration clearly affirms the equal dignity and rights of women and men as human persons and as Christians, citing Gal. 3:28; at the same time it insists on the influence of sex on the proper identity of the person, and the value and importance of sexual differentiation for the human community. It maintains that "equality is in no way identity."[27] So, the Declaration rejects the notion

---

[24]   Introduction, 519.

[25]   Art. 2, 520; Commentary, 526.

[26]   According to the Commentary, 529, "We have already discarded a fair number of explanations given by mediaeval theologians." These are described as defective because they rely on a theory of women's inferiority and state of subjection to men.

[27]   Art. 6, 523.

that sexual differentiation implies hierarchical ordering, but envisions the sexes as complementary.

Third, the Declaration does not derive its fundamental argument from the analogy of faith, that is, from a consideration of the doctrine of God, Christology, soteriology, the consequences of baptismal equality, or the representative character of the ministerial priesthood. It appeals instead to history and to precedent—the precedent by which Jesus chose twelve men and gave the apostolic charge to them and not to his women disciples.

The Declaration distinguished between the foundation or "essential reason" for its judgment—discovered not in an explicit saying of Jesus but in his example, interpreted through subsequent decisions of the Church when faced with contrary practice—and the theological reasons advanced to explain it. Among these latter, referred to as the arguments from fittingness, it includes reasoning based on the symbolism of sexual difference in biblical revelation, and the question of the sacramental representation of God, Christ, and the Church. By locating these in the second part of the Declaration, the authors signal that this reasoning is not thought to provide a demonstrative argument but only an illustration by means of the analogy of faith.

This is the crux of the difference between our two ways of examining the question. The official Roman Catholic explanation rests on the example of Jesus, believed to express his will for the Church. That this choice of twelve men was deliberate, that it was not related only to the role of the twelve patriarchs of Israel, that the exclusion of women was not due to religious or socio-cultural constraints, that the Twelve actually constitute the normative expression of the apostolic ministry for the future of the Church, even when the "Twelve" and the "apostles" are not co-extensive New Testament categories, and even when the relation of their office to the priestly ministry which took shape in the Church of the second century is difficult to trace—all of these are the questions the Roman Catholic explanation raises as fundamental.

In March, 1978 a special joint international consultation on the ordination of women cosponsored by the Anglican Consultative Council and the Secretariat for Promoting Christian Unity was held in Versailles.[28] The Versailles Consultation situated the "new obstacle" to reconciliation of ministries within the framework of doctrinal development. Members noted that the Roman Catholic Church did not, in asserting the tradition, affirm it as a matter of divine law. They took hope from the fact that Anglican churches which had proceeded to ordain women to the presbyterate were confident that they had not departed from the understanding of apostolic ministry expressed in the Canterbury Statement. They recommended dialogue on

---

[28] "Women Priests: Ecumenical Obstacle?" *Origins* 6 (September 21, 1978), 211–12.

the related questions of human sexuality, culture and tradition, and freedom and authority. Still, they did not shrink from stating the problem in words that continue to describe our dilemma:

Because of their mutual esteem neither communion can take lightly the fact that the other seems either to do something not warranted by the will of Christ or to be lacking in sensitivity to the promptings of the Holy Spirit.[29]

As the Archbishop of Canterbury prepared for the 1978 Lambeth Conference, the ecumenical counsel he received from the Roman Catholic Church was clear. Addressing a special hearing on the question in the name of the Secretariat for Promoting Christian Unity, Bishop Cahal Brendan Daly repeated the Vatican position at the Lambeth Conference.[30] He explained that the doctrinal tradition was not "inert," and was not simply an unexamined way of acting, but "one so firm and decisive as not to have needed formulation or defence." He proposed that the burden of proof lay with those who would depart from the long-standing practice "founded on Christ's example." He also cautioned that despite press reports which portrayed this decision as provisional, the firmness of the Roman Catholic position could not be called into question. He repeated the judgment that departure from the tradition would constitute a "new and grave problem."

The 1978 Lambeth Conference, in resolution 21, noted that four member churches had ordained women priests and eight others had agreed or approved this in principle, finding no theological objections; still, other member churches either remained undecided or stated that they held fundamental objections to this move.[31] Resolution 22 acknowledged that "member churches might wish to consecrate a woman to the episcopate," and urged consultation and prudence "lest the bishop's office should become a cause of disunity instead of a focus of unity."

C. The Third Phase: 1982–86

The third phase of this discussion is marked by some clarification and assessment of the Anglican approach.

ARCIC's *Final Report,* released in 1981, did not formally investigate the ordination of women.[32] The "Observations" on this report released by the Congregation of the Doctrine of the Faith, however, assert that the

---

[29]   *Ibid.,* no. 5.
[30]   "The Lambeth Conference/Three Resolutions," *Origins* 8 (September 21, 1978), 213–14. Bishop Daly's testimony is quoted in the margins of the text.
[31]   *Ibid.*
[32]   Anglican-Roman Catholic International Commission, *The Final Report* (Cincinnati: Forward Movement Publications, 1982).

"new canonical regulations . . . introduced . . . in some parts of the Anglican Communion . . . are formally opposed to the 'common traditions' of the two communions and therefore create an obstacle of a doctrinal character," an obstacle evidently thought to affect the solidity of the convergence.[33] ARCIC-II, constituted by the Archbishop of Canterbury and Pope John Paul II in 1982, was charged with studying "all that hinders the mutual recognition of the ministries of our two communions."[34]

In the meantime, ARC-USA had already undertaken to study several subjects which it hoped would establish a common context: "the church's teaching about human sexuality and marriage, the role of Mary in the life, devotion, and theology of the church, and the admission of women to the ordained ministry."[35] Released in 1984, the ARC-USA document, "Images of God: Reflections on Christian Anthropology," attempted to state a consensus and to follow up the idea that a development of doctrine, given impetus by Christian feminism, sheds new light on women's ability to represent God, Christ, and the Church. "Images of God" reported a divergence of opinion—not always according to church allegiance—on the theological significance of Jesus' maleness and on three models for the understanding of the relationship of man and woman and the consequences of each.[36]

"Images of God" affirmed the doctrine of ministry and ordination adopted in the *Final Report*, but acknowledged disagreement as to "whether a woman may be ordained to 'stand in sacramental relation to Christ himself'" in the special case of eucharistic presidency.[37] ARC-USA states the Vatican's position very concisely; it is chiefly concerned to respond to its theological reasoning, especially to the argument that natural resemblance between the priest and Christ requires a male priesthood. Countering this, it reports that Episcopalians who support the ordination of women hold that the priest is an image of Christ by virtue of what he or she is and does as a person baptized and ordained with the power of the Spirit, not by virtue of male sexuality. They advance a positive case also: women's gifts will enrich the priesthood, and "the ordination of women serves to protect the doctrine of God and Christology from an imbalance which diminishes Christian revelation and keeps women relatively unequal as members of the

---

[33] "Observations on the ARCIC Final Report," *Origins* 11 (May 6, 1982), 752–56, at 754. These observations twice raise the problem of "adopting as the effective norm for reading the scriptures only what historical criticism maintains, thus allowing the homogeneity of the developments which appear in tradition to remain in doubt" (*ibid.*).

[34] "The Pope and Canterbury's Archbishop: A Joint Statement," *Origins* 12 (June 10, 1982), 49, 51, at 51.

[35] "Images of God, Reflections on Christian Anthropology," *Origins* 13 (January 5, 1984), 505-12, at 505.

[36] *Ibid.*, nos. 14 and 45–48.

[37] *Ibid.*, no. 62.

Church."[38] The section on the ordination of women concludes with a recommendation for further studies on "the nature of representational imagery, especially as it applies to the eucharist and the ordained ministry."[39]

Debate on women's access to priesthood in the General Synod of the
Church of England in 1984 prompted Pope John Paul II to initiate correspondence with the Archbishop of Canterbury, Robert Runcie. In a letter
dated December 20, 1984, he states that "the increase in the number of
Anglican Churches which admit, or are preparing to admit, women to
priestly ordination constitutes, in the eyes of the Catholic Church, an increasingly serious obstacle" to the progress already made.[40]

The Archbishop of Canterbury took counsel with the primates of the
Anglican Communion and replied the following December. His letter al-
ludes to "the serious doctrinal reasons" that motivate those who favor the
change in practice.[41] Dr. Runcie explained these serious doctrinal reasons in
a letter to Cardinal Willebrands, president of the Secretariat for Promoting
Christian Unity and Cardinal Willebrands replied at some length.[42] This
published correspondence constitutes the most explicit formal exchange
concerning the arguments pro and con at the international level.

According to the Archbishop, Anglicans who see no reasons against
change argue as follows: (1) Scripture and Tradition present no fundamental
objection; (2) by itself, the witness of the New Testament does not permit
a clear settlement of the question; (3) Tradition appears to be "open to this
development, because the exclusion of women from priestly ministry cannot
be proved to be of 'divine law.'"[43] In addition, they believe there are com-
pelling doctrinal reasons for the development of the Tradition in this direction. The "most substantial" reason, which seems not only to justify but even
to require the ordination of women, is Christological. The Eternal Word
assumed our human flesh, redeemed it and has taken it up into the life of
the Trinity. If women are sharers in this new life, it must be because Christ's
humanity is "inclusive of women." Second, because the priest represents the
priestly nature of Christ's body, the Church—especially in the eucharistic
presidency—stands in a special sacramental relationship with Christ, whose
humanity includes both male and female, women should be ordained. In
this way Christ's inclusive High Priesthood will be more perfectly represented; in fact, the representative nature of the ministerial priesthood is
weakened by an exclusively male priesthood.

In reply, Cardinal Willebrands reiterates the Catholic Church's con-

---

[38]   *Ibid.,* nos. 66–67.
[39]   *Ibid.,* no. 68.
[40]   "Women's Ordination and the Progress of Ecumenism," *Origins* 16 (July 17, 1986), 153,
155–60, at 155.
[41]   *Ibid.,* 155.
[42]   *Ibid.,* 156–58.
[43]   *Ibid.,* 156.

viction that it is not authorized to admit women to priestly ordination, citing as his principal reason the constant Tradition of ordaining only men to the presbyterate and episcopate. The Catholic Church "has considered the practice of Christ and the Apostles a norm from which she could not deviate."[44] Urging that the matter be taken up by ARCIC-II and that the Anglican Communion not make so radical a departure "alone" because of the serious ecclesiological implications, the cardinal then indicates what he regards as unsatisfactory in the case put by the archbishop.

In the first place, he notes that ARCIC's *Final Report* advances a common understanding of ministerial priesthood, and cautions that "the question of who can or cannot be ordained may not be separated from its appropriate context of sacramental theology and ecclesiology."[45] Priesthood, exercised by bishops with priests as their co-workers, is an essential element in the constitution of the Church and the means by which the redemptive work of Christ (his once-for-all sacrifice) is made a present reality. There is, he affirms, a "real continuity" between Christ's saving work and the priestly office. Second, asking whether the place of the ordained ministry in the divine economy of salvation is adequately reflected in the Anglican case, the cardinal reviews the biblical imagery which draws on the symbolism of human sexuality in its portrayal of the divine-human relation. He asserts that the representative role of the ministerial priesthood is understood with reference to Christ's role as Head of the Church. The restriction of priesthood to males, he states, has to be understood in relation to the Savior's male identity and to the priest's iconic role of acting *in persona Christi.* "The priest represents Christ in his saving relationship with his body, the church. He does not primarily represent the priesthood of the whole people of God."[46] He states frankly that the Anglican arguments "do not negotiate the manifold theological issues which this matter raises," and therefore do not, in his judgment, justify the radical innovation of admitting women to priesthood.

D. The Fourth Phase: 1988–92

In the fourth phase of this history, there is a marked shift of emphasis, with new attention being given to the Roman Catholic approach. This is now correlated with concern for the ecclesiological implications of the ordination of women not only as priests but as bishops. In my judgment, this phase reveals the link between this question and the unresolved issues of ARCIC's work on Authority in the Church.

The bishops of the 1988 Lambeth Conference acknowledged that

---

[44] *Ibid.*, 159. Here, Willebrands refers to articles 1–4 of *Inter insigniores.*
[45] *Ibid.*, 160.
[46] *Ibid.*

member churches of the Anglican Communion would continue to determine their own policy regarding the ordination of women to the priesthood,
and that in a number of provinces their consecration to the episcopate was
also a distinct possibility.[47] They committed themselves to continue in communion even if the communion suffered some impairment due to divergent
positions on this question.

In a letter to Pope John Paul II, written in August, 1988, but released
later,[48] Archbishop Robert Runcie expressed his conviction that the principal issue facing Lambeth 1988 was "the underlying question of authority,
the developing tradition of the church and ecclesiology." In the judgment of
the conference, a schism in the Anglican Communion was a greater threat
than impaired communion. Once again, the archbishop wrote of his desire
for an ecumenical "debate" on the divisive issue of the ordination of women.
He said the Anglican Communion's positive response to the ARCIC agreed
statements on eucharist and ordained ministry was a significant step toward
the mutual recognition of ministries, but acknowledged that "there will be
no easy solution to the difficult question of the ordination of women."

In reply, Pope John Paul II recognized, on the one hand, the positive
signs of "openness to fuller communion with the Catholic Church" evident
in Lambeth's response to ARCIC's *Final Report,* but expressed concern, on
the other, over developments which "seem to have placed new obstacles in
the way of reconciliation between Catholics and Anglicans."[49] It was in this
letter that he made the comment cited earlier:

The ordination of women to the priesthood in some provinces of the Anglican
Communion, together with the recognition of the right of individual provinces to
proceed with the ordination of women to the episcopacy, appears to pre-empt
[ARCIC-II's] study and effectively block the path to the mutual recognition of
ministries.

He reaffirmed the Catholic Church's opposition to this development,
calling it "a break with tradition of a kind we have no competence to
authorize," and urged that the ecumenical and ecclesiological aspects of the
question be given further attention to prevent "a serious erosion" of the
communion already possessed.

During a visit to the Vatican in autumn of 1992, Archbishop Runcie and

---

[47] *The Truth Shall Make You Free: The Lambeth Conference 1988* (London: Anglican
Consultative Council, 1988). See Resolution 1: The Ordination or Consecration of Women to
the Episcopate. The Section Report on Mission and Ministry acknowledges that "it may be
many years before the Anglican Communion can be said to be of a single mind regarding the
ordination of women" (nos. 132–150, at 138).

[48] "Letters Exchanged by Pope and Canterbury Archbishop," *Origins* 19 (June 8, 1989),
63–64.

[49] *Ibid.,* 64.

the Pope issued a Common Statement expressing their concern that divergence on this issue prevents reconciliation and reflects "important ecclesiological differences."[50] The 1991 Report of ARCIC-II, "Church as Communion," can be read as an effort to address the ecclesiological question in order to develop an approach to this "unresolved matter."[51]

The Catholic Church's official response to the *Final Report* of ARCIC-I, released in December, 1991[52] challenged the Commission's view that agreement could be reached without asking who can or cannot be ordained. According to the Response, "the question of the subject of ordination is linked with the nature of the sacrament of holy orders."[53]

ARCIC's "Clarifications of Certain Aspects of the Agreed Statements on Eucharist and Ministry," submitted to the Vatican in September, 1993 acknowledges this judgment but maintains that this issue "involves far more than the question of ministry as such. It raises profound questions of ecclesiology and authority in relation to Tradition."[54] Thus, this belongs to the current mandate of ARCIC-II.

This backward glance over the twenty or so years this discussion has gone on reveals, I believe, the two different approaches. The Anglican approach finds in Scripture and Tradition no obstacles to a change. Since the only serious objection posed up until now was based upon a faulty view of women, this cannot constitute a theological tradition but only a way of acting determined by socio-cultural norms. Once this faulty view is rejected, the way is open to a new development. Recognition of women's equality—the new anthropology—in fact requires this development when correlated with the doctrine of God, Christology, soteriology, and the priest's role as representative of Christ and of the Church.

The Ordination of Women to the Priesthood, a Second Report by the House of Bishops of the General Synod of the Church of England (June, 1988) confirms that this approach provides the framework for that Church's discussion pro and con.[55] Arguments presented in favor of ordaining women identify the all-male priesthood as a counter-sign to the truth of the Gospel which threatens the mission and unity of the Church and reinforces patterns of inequality and alienation. An inclusive priesthood, on the contrary, would witness clearly not only to the equality and dignity of women and men but

[50] "A Meeting of the Pope and Canterbury's Archbishop," *Origins* 19 (October 12, 1989), 316–17.
[51] "Church as Communion," *Catholic International* 2 (14 April 1991), 327–38.
[52] "Vatican Responds to ARCIC-I Final Report," *Origins* 21 (December 19, 1991), 441, 443–47.
[53] *Ibid.,* 446.
[54] Here I break sequence, to indicate ARCIC's answer to the Vatican Response: "Vatican Says Clarifications Strengthen Agreement," *Origins* 24 (October 6, 1994), 299–304, at 304.
[55] *The Ordination of Women to the Priesthood,* A Second Report by the House of Bishops GS 829 (London: General Synod of the Church of England, 1988).

to the mystery of the Trinity and to the Church as a place where the kingdom is being born.[56] Arguments advanced against the ordination of women appeal to the Church's long tradition but also to the revelation of God signified in the particularity of Jesus' maleness, the male priesthood as most faithfully representing the priesthood of Christ, and the role and status of men in Creation and Redemption. Male headship and the proper sub-ordination of women are mentioned as offering an important witness to society today, and the preservation of the male priesthood is held up as a powerful witness to the continuity of the Church's ministry.[57]

Views both pro and con take the new situation as a starting point, and then take a stand on what fidelity to the Gospel requires. The presentation in the House of Bishops' report has as its chief reference point the questions which *Inter insigniores* regards as belonging to the theological arguments from fittingness. Although attention is given to the Church's tradition, no evidence is provided with respect to the prohibition of ordaining women.[58] The question of Jesus' choice of twelve men finds no place in the House of Bishops' Report, despite the fact that the Roman Catholic Church has repeatedly identified this as the "fundamental reason."

By contrast, the Roman Catholic approach—at least since *Inter insigniores*—takes a different starting point. It relies very explicitly on the fact that Jesus himself chose twelve men; that—given his freedom with respect to the conventions of his time—he could have included women but did not; that his example was followed in the apostolic Church, despite the active participation of women in various ministries; and that subsequent genera-tions carefully maintained this pattern and condemned contrary practice. Appeal to the subordinate status of women, often cited on behalf of this tradition, is abandoned as a supporting reason[59]; appeal to Jesus' example and that of the apostles is accepted. The questions which lead Anglicans to revise their practice are not ignored, but they are regarded as arguments from fittingness. They are not thought capable of demonstrating the fact, nor of disproving it. Therefore, the concrete facts of salvation history are given priority, and they are seen to be essentially related to the constitution of the Church. In any of its official correspondence with the Anglican Communion, appeal is made only to this line of reasoning.

---

[56] *Ibid.*, no. 163. See no. 151 with reference to the hermeneutic of tradition.
[57] *Ibid.*, no. 162.
[58] *Ibid.*, nos. 149–55. In fact, no. 152 asserts that "in spite of [the Church's] positive view of women there was no challenge made until now to an all male priesthood." The Declaration *Inter insigniores*, on the contrary, proposes that the tradition has been established in response to such challenges (art. 1). This point calls for further joint investigation.
[59] Pope John Paul II's apostolic letter *Mulieris dignitatem* provides an exposition which reinterprets New Testament teaching on "subordination" in light of Gal. 3:28, the "Gospel innovation." The text, "On the Dignity and Vocation of Women," is in *Origins* 18 (October 6, 1988), 261, 263–83.

The 1992 Vote of the Church of England, *Ordinatio sacerdotalis* and the Way Forward

The vote of the Church of England's General Synod on November 11, 1992, opening the way to the ordination of women to the priesthood in the spring of 1994, provoked a most serious crisis in our progress towards the reconciliation of ministries. Because the Archbishop of Canterbury as primate of all England exercises a certain primacy among the bishops of the Anglican Communion, the Roman Catholic Church regards the decision of this Church with special concern. Many who wait for the full communion of Anglicans and Roman Catholics received the news of the General Synod's vote with heavy hearts, aware of its implications.

Pope John Paul II's apostolic letter on Priestly Ordination[60] was addressed to the bishops of his own Church, not to Anglicans, but it can be seen as reinforcing the distinctive Roman Catholic approach. In recalling the "fundamental reasons" which prohibit the ordination of women, the Pope asserts that Christ gave the Church "her fundamental constitution, her theological anthropology." "The Church," he writes, "has always acknowledged as a perennial norm her Lord's way of acting in choosing the twelve men whom he made the foundation of his Church."[61] By Jesus' choice these men did not only receive a function but were associated with him in his own mission. The Apostles followed the same pattern in choosing their co-workers, men who would carry on their mission of representing the Lord.[62]

The Pope also repeats the ancient argument that the exclusion of women from priestly ordination "cannot mean that women are of lesser dignity, nor can it be construed as discrimination against them,"[63] since even the Lord's own Mother was not called to the mission proper to the apostles nor to the ministerial priesthood.

This forceful appeal not just to the unbroken Tradition but to its foundation, traced to the will of Christ revealed in his choice of the Twelve, is more than a reiteration of the "fundamental reasons" given in 1975. In my opinion, it represents an effort to direct attention *away* from arguments drawn primarily from the analogy of faith—speculative efforts to discover what arrangement might best witness to the "inclusive" message of the Gospel—and *towards* the prior fact that ordained ministry originates with

---

[60]   *Origins* 24 (June 9, 1994), 49, 51–52.
[61]   *Ibid.*, no. 2, 51.
[62]   See Albert Vanhoye, "Church's practice in continuity with New Testament teaching," *L'Osservatore Romano* 10 (10 March 1993), 10–11, for an updated version of the case made by *Inter insigniores*. See also no. 1577 of the *Catechism of the Catholic Church* which explicitly links the college of the twelve apostles to the college of bishops in its statement of reason for the tradition.
[63]   *Ibid.*, no. 3.

the Church itself, and is given its shape by Christ. Shortly after the apostolic letter appeared, Cardinal Ratzinger wrote that the Pope wished to emphasize the limits to the Church's authority by calling attention to the will of Christ, and that he leaves the task of elaborating the anthropological implications of this choice to theologians.[64]

What is the problem? As debate within the Roman Catholic Church and between our two communions has proceeded, some theologians (both Roman Catholic and Anglican) have dismissed the appeal to the example of Jesus and the apostles in a way which would, if carried to its logical conclusion, undermine our common ecclesiology. Arguments put forth in favor of ordaining women, because they are based on the doctrine of baptismal equality, tend to call into question the real distinction between the common priesthood of the baptized and the ministerial priesthood. They often suppose that arrangements for ministry in the early Church were worked out without reference to what Jesus did in his earthly life, especially to his choice and commission of the Twelve. But this bears directly on an understanding of the constitution of the Church.

The Vatican Response to the *Final Report,* it seems to me, continues to set our agenda. The questions this agenda requires us to address, or to reaffirm, are: (1) the dominical foundation and sacramental nature of the ministerial priesthood, (2) the ministerial priesthood as an essential element in the Church, (3) the sacramental distinction between the ministerial priesthood and the common priesthood of the baptized which it serves, (4) the functions of the ministerial priesthood as a continuation of Christ's ministry, (5) the historical continuity between the apostolic ministry and the episcopal office (apostolic succession), and (6) the role of the Tradition and the Church's teaching authority in the interpretation of the Scriptures. It would not be difficult to find formal expressions of our common belief on all of these matters in the *Final Report,* as ARCIC's *Clarifications* of 1993 demonstrates, but it remains necessary to make their implications for this topic explicit.

These questions are not new to our dialogue. But they need to be revisited and set in clear relationship with the issues left unresolved in ARCIC's Agreed Statement on Authority in the Church. The same hermeneutical questions are at stake: How assess the position of Peter among the apostles as attested by the Petrine texts? How explain the transmission of Peter's leadership to the bishop of Rome? How discern which ecclesial institutions are of divine right? What is the source of the pastoral authority needed to exercise *episcopé?* On what basis does the episcopal ministry claim to teach with a special authority and to be competent to make deci-

---

[64]   Joseph Ratzinger, "The Limits of Church Authority," *L'Osservatore Romano* 26 (29 June 1994), 6–8, no. 2, at 6.

sions that become part of the Church's permanent witness? By what process does an authentic development in the Church's teaching take place and according to what criteria may it be rejected or verified? Indeed, this topic does raise "profound questions of ecclesiology and authority in relation to Tradition."[65]

The common foundation on which we move towards fuller consensus on these matters, in addition to "the Gospels and the ancient common traditions,"[66] is our commitment to the historic episcopate as a gift of the Spirit, an institution that belongs to God's plan for his Church. I believe that commitment to this strong foundation, and renewed attention to the very questions which have been part of our agenda for years, must give direction to the future of our dialogue on the ordination of women.

Postscript

Since this paper was written, the Congregation for the Doctrine of the Faith, with the approval of the Pope, reasserted *Ordinatio sacerdotalis* in the form of a reply to the *dubium* concerning that letter's teaching.[67] The reply clarifies the reason for which the prior teaching is said to require definitive assent. The teaching in question is that "the Church has no authority whatsoever to confer priestly ordination on women." The reason it is said to require definitive assent is that, "founded on the written word of God, and from the beginning constantly preserved and applied in the tradition of the Church, it has been set forth infallibly by the ordinary and universal magisterium." Pope John Paul II, by a formal declaration, hands this same teaching on as something that belongs to the deposit of the faith. What some have continued to regard as a question of discipline, subject to development in light of recent teaching on the equality of women, is hereby expressly affirmed to be a question of doctrine, and even to have been taught infallibly by the ordinary and universal magisterium. This new development places squarely before Anglicans and Roman Catholics the agenda outlined in the preceding paragraphs, especially the "profound questions of ecclesiology and authority in relation to Tradition."

---

[65] ARCIC's "Clarifications," (cited in n. 56), 304.
[66] According to its original mandate, the work of ARCIC is to be founded on these.
[67] "Inadmissibility of Women to Ministerial Priesthood," *Origins* 25:24 (November 30, 1995), 401, 403. It was prompted by "a number of problematic and negative statements" from certain theologians, organizations or priests and religious, and associations of lay people. See "Cardinal Ratzinger: Cover Letter to Bishops' Conference Presidents," *ibid.*, p. 403.

A Response to Papers on *Apostolicae Curae*

JOANNE MCWILLIAM*

It seems to me, reviewing the papers we have, that Professor Tavard at the beginning and Professor Butler near the end each put a finger on two key issues underlying (but not far under) the non-recognition of Anglican orders by the Roman Catholic Church: different understanding of tradition in the two churches and different models of decision making. The two issues are clearly and closely connected but I will address only the first. To what degree is the past normative and how is the past brought into the present?

The past and tradition are not, of course, convertible terms. Tradition can be understood as that part of the past which the Christian community *chooses* to preserve as normative—in some cases even authoritative—for the present. Not only has that part of the past deemed worthy of such preservation been differently assessed, but the basis of that assessment has been as divisive as the doctrines or institutions deriving from it.

I very much appreciated Canon Hill's point that tradition can be centred on the past or on the future. Too commonly the focus has been on the first to the neglect of the second. Professor Tavard, for example, demonstrated that the understanding of tradition implicit in *Apostolicae curae* narrowed it to precedent. He mentioned the context of the modernist controversy in which the encyclical was written, that the ideologies of the late nineteenth century in all their variety were seen by Rome as a "conspiracy to ruin the church." I wish more had been made of this climate of fear and its consequences. It is hard for us to imagine, a century later, the ecclesial paranoia of the times. The Anglican Church, too, had its modernist crisis, but it was a relatively mild one—relative, that is, to the Roman Catholic upheaval from which that Church is still scarred.

It is in the consideration of history and tradition that the hermeneutical concept of "horizons" is helpful. Historical understanding must grasp the particular historical horizon out of which a tradition speaks, otherwise we risk misunderstanding that tradition. And, having understood it as best we can, we are able to see historical continuity not as inhibiting, but rather as "a transmission generative of meaning."

Tradition has never in Christian history been free of criticism. The

* Joanne McWilliam is Mary Crooke Hoffman Professor of Theology at the General Theological Seminary in New York, and formerly Professor of Theology at Trinity College, Toronto.

attitude of Christians to the legacy of their past has never been one of uncritical acceptance of the whole. "Only the living tradition can sort out the many traditions inherited from the past" (Tavard). And Augustine stated baldly (this may surprise some) that when tradition and truth are in conflict, truth must prevail. Generally this tension was implicit, expressed in selection: what should be retained, what discarded?

The New Testament authors were variously selective in their use of the Hebrew scriptures. The New Testament books themselves went in and out of favour with different churches until the canon was fixed in the late fourth century. And we are selective in what we take from the New Testament as authoritative. That Christ ordained only Jews (if, indeed, he ordained anybody) is generally acknowledged and its implications generally ignored.

An understanding of tradition oriented to the past will see it open to criticism only in terms of the past. "[W]here a tradition has been established on the basis of a historical event, and where this historical event is also accorded permanent significance, the norm of possible criticism of tradition must be primarily only the 'return to the source', the investigation of what was originally experienced, done and meant" (Karl-Heinz Weger, "Tradition", *Sacramentum Mundi* 6. Karl Rahner *et al.* eds. New York: Herder and Herder, 1970, p. 271).

To see a tradition as "unalterable" because it has its origin in divine revelation seems to me to confine God to the past. Professor Tavard reminds us that reception is "an integral moment" in the transmission of tradition. In looking at the reception of our selected tradition we can return to the language of horizons. The horizon of our present is always being formed insofar as we are constantly testing our judgments against (among other things) tradition. To receive and appropriate a tradition is to expand our horizon of the present by fusing it with one of the past. In doing so, both change. And with that change we move into living tradition which recognizes the presence of the Spirit in the present as well as the past and which looks to the future. Let us call it visionary tradition.

Canon Hill has suggested that the question of apostolic succession can be seen in this way—eschatologically as well as historically—as the final gathering as well as the initial commissioning. I think it unwise, in any case, to try to build the validity of orders on an unbroken succession from Peter or from the apostles generally. It is far from proven. The apostolic succession in eschatological context would be, as Canon Hill says, "dangerously ecumenically liberating." I see visionary tradition also in Professor Bradshaw's paper as he urges us to change our focus from the essential words and specific moments in liturgical rites to the ritual as a whole. In my own field of systematic theology, we see the same sort of change as we increasingly talk of the "Christ event." Equally liberating is the fact, alluded to by Professor Yarnold, that the Porvoo agreement recognized that a continuity of oversight, including the occasional consecration of bishops by presbyters, honours the episcopal tradition and has precedents in the patristic and medieval church.

I think it unfortunate that the papers are to some degree diverted into the question of the ordination of women. The question of the validity of Anglican orders and the rightness or wrongness of ordaining women are distinguishable. Are Anglican orders valid? Should they be conferred on women? The Roman Catholic church could—in theory—answer "yes" to the first question and "no" to the second. But to do so would be inconsistent. If I hear the situation correctly, it seems that the Roman Catholic church has rejected both for the same (ostensible) reason—the understanding of tradition only as precedent. If this understanding of tradition is the real, and not only the ostensible reason, then to change one judgment would involve—if consistency is a factor—changing both. In such a scenario, the ordination of women would not be a further obstacle to reconciliation. But if, in the case of the ordination of women, precedent is only an ostensible reason, then Anglican women in orders would be an added obstacle to reconciliation. To paraphrase Canon Hill, non-recognition of the rightness of ordaining women would be a symptom, not a cause of our differences.

The Dimension of Ecumenical Consensus in the Revision of Anglican Ordination Rites: A Response to Professor Paul Bradshaw

J. ROBERT WRIGHT*

What sort of ecumenical consensus should be necessary before a church decides to revise its ordination rites? This is the question that posed itself to me as I read Paul Bradshaw's incisive essay, "The Liturgical Consequences of *Apostolicae curae* for Anglican Ordination Rites," to which I have been invited to respond. My admiration of Professor Bradshaw's liturgical scholarship is already on record in the very positive review I have published of his *Ordination Rites of the Ancient Churches of East and West* in 1995 in the *Cistercian Studies Quarterly.* Now my task in this essay will be to probe the ecumenical dimension of the position he has taken in his essay in the present volume, and in particular to ask what sort of consensus might be necessary before the Anglican churches could adopt and move forward with his proposals? Is there a dimension of consensus to his proposals, even an ecumenical dimension especially between Anglicans and the Church of Rome, that has not yet been addressed as thoroughly as it should be?

For Professor Bradshaw's proposals to take hold, a basic agreement would have to be reached on several points, each of which I shall now discuss more or less in the order in which he mentions them:

First, it would be necessary for Anglicans generally to agree with him that it is "troubling" that the ordination rites in the Church of England's *Alternative Service Book 1980* were drafted in the shadow of *Apostolicae curae,* and that it is even "more troubling" that, as he asserts, the Anglican liturgical revisers as recently as 1980 were willing to accept what he labels as "the scholastic approach to the essentials of ordination" merely in order to appease the Church of Rome when they should have known better. He may be correct that this is what happened in England at that time, but I am not sure that all Anglicans would agree with his value judgment and see that action as "troubling," even in view of the rather strained relations that exist between the Anglican Communion and the Church of Rome today. It may

---

* J. Robert Wright is St. Mark's-in-the-Bowery Professor of Ecclesiastical History at the General Theological Seminary. He has been a member of the second Anglican-Roman Catholic International Commission, and he is theological consultant to the Ecumenical Office of the Episcopal Church in the United States.

rather have been the case, as I suspect, that the Anglican revisers in 1980 knew full well what they were doing, even if they were not advocating a return to a patristic model, but that they acted more out of an ecumenical respect for the Roman Church rather than out of fear for Rome's shadow. There is always a tension between the ideal and the practical, and they may well have felt that their "firm desire to make twentieth-century revisions of Anglican ordination rites impregnable," as he describes it, was justified in view of the ecumenical consensus with Rome that existed even then. Can it be proven that this consensus among Anglican liturgical experts has now shifted from what it was in 1980, to the position advocated by Dr. Bradshaw in this essay in 1995?

The second prerequisite necessary for Dr. Bradshaw's proposals to take hold is that there must be some general agreement with him that the view of E.C. Ratcliff which so dominated Anglican thinking about ordination rites in the middle of this century is wrong, namely that "the substantive clause of the Ordination Prayer was a petition asking God to send his Holy Spirit upon the person being ordained to make him a Bishop (or Priest or Deacon)." Bradshaw cites impressive evidence of the influence of Ratcliff's views upon the Church of England and other related churches, in the revisions of whose rites he says that "Anglican concerns about the validity of ordinations were obviously a major factor in their compilation," and he cites evidence also of the remarkable correspondence of Ratcliff's thought with that underlying revisions of ordination rites in the Roman Catholic Church as recently as 1968. Even if these concerns of Ratcliff and others did influence Anglican revisions, and I suspect that Bradshaw is right about this, it is nonetheless obvious that Roman Catholic liturgical revisions of the same period could not have been under the same influence. It will therefore be necessary, if Bradshaw's position is to be sustained, to produce reasons to show why the Roman Catholic revisions of the same period did not take the view that he seems to think Anglicans then would have taken if they were not under the shadow of Rome. Evidence also needs to be given of other Anglican liturgiologists besides himself, and I suspect there are some, who agree with his position. Even more to the point, if we are to think of Anglicans and Roman Catholics as sister churches, evidence will have to be adduced to show that a consensus in the Roman Church is also moving away from its traditional understanding of ordination and in the direction of that of Professor Bradshaw.

Next, it will be necessary to convince other scholars that the views Dr. Bradshaw attributes to Ratcliff, as well as what he describes as the dominant tradition in the Church of Rome (namely, that ordination rites should include the imposition of hands during an ordination prayer asking God to send the Holy Spirit upon the ordinand and make that person a bishop or priest or deacon, and that the central petition of the ordination prayer alone should be repeated where there is more than one person to be ordained) are anachronistic, medieval or even post-medieval, and incapable of withstanding his scholarly "scrutiny" (as he puts it). It is one thing to assert on historical grounds that such ordination rites are not patristic, and here I suspect there should be widespread agreement since Bradshaw himself is a leading authority on what the ancient texts contained. It is quite another thing to assert on theological grounds that if some practice of the present church can not be firmly located in the patristic church it should therefore be eliminated. His position demands consensus on this principle, and for it to be accepted there must be a conversion to it of those who for various reasons would prefer the practice and thought of some later century, as well as of those who would want to turn the clock back even further than Bradshaw and who would assert that because ordination itself cannot be found in the New Testament there is no need for it today. Many would assume that, for a Christian practice to be proven as "primitive" (his word about what is desirable), it must go behind the patristic period to the New Testament itself, whereas there are many others who would say that "primitiveness" is not the touchstone by which every liturgical revision should be judged.

Bradshaw buttresses his position with a fourth point that is also, as yet, lacking much consensus: that there should be no specific "moment" of ordination in the ordination prayer because there should be no specific "moment" of consecration within the Eucharistic prayer. As evidence that Anglicans may agree with this view about the Eucharist he cites a disparate collection of authorities consisting of Herbert Thorndike from the seventeenth century, a committee report presented to (but not adopted by) the 1958 Lambeth Conference, the eucharistic rite in the Church of England's draft Series 3, and the views of the English Anglican evangelical Bishop Colin Buchanan. No doubt a few other modern Anglican liturgiologists could be found who would agree with this view of the Eucharist, but such evidence will need to be gathered and set down in print in order to convince people that it is a "trend," as Bradshaw asserts. Furthermore, it will be necessary to show that, in spite of much good modern Eucharistic theology from the pens of such writers as Professor Bradshaw himself, those who wish to retain the "specific" words and actions within the Eucharistic prayer that he finds to betray a "scholastic" outlook really wish to retain a "moment of consecration" rather than, in doing so, merely to retain a focus of devotion without which there would be a void. Granted what Vatican II and some eminent contemporary Roman Catholic liturgiologists are saying about the progressive realization of the presence of Christ in the Eucharist, why has the Roman Catholic Church not abolished the words and actions in its Eucharistic prayers that still allow for a focus of devotion? And why has the Episcopal Church, without the vocal protest of its own liturgiologists, voted as recently as its 1979 Prayer Book that additional elements may be "consecrated" by a formula that includes only the epiclesis and the words of institution (page 408)? What is more conducive to belief in a "moment of consecration" than this formula, and why was it added, not abolished, in the 1979 Book if there is really a "trend" in the opposite direction?

Professor Bradshaw faces the problem of what to do about a "moment of ordination" when there is more than one candidate to be ordained at the same time by giving his opinion that "Fortunately, in many parts of the world this now occurs less frequently than it used to do because of the decrease in the number of ordinands" and then adding his advice that single candidates should be ordained in local congregations rather than "retaining the medieval custom of ordaining at some more central location for the convenience of the ordaining bishop." Here too, of course, evidence of an emerging and ecumenical consensus will be needed, both to show agreement that the decrease in the number of ordinands is in fact widely regarded as "fortunate" (his word) and also to show that the churches, both Anglican and Roman Catholic, now admit that they were ordaining at central locations such as cathedrals merely for the convenience of the ordaining bishop and not rather in order to make a theological point about the centrality of the historic episcopate and of the diocesan cathedral in the church's life.

At the end of Professor Bradshaw's essay we come to his final conclusion for the problem of Anglican orders, the solution that he presumably hopes other Anglican liturgiologists and indeed the whole Anglican Communion will accept on patristic, i.e. primitive, grounds, and which he hopes will also commend itself as a basis for radical revision of ordination rites in the Roman Catholic Church as well, after which the problem of Anglican orders should be solved. What is this solution, and does it have the potential for achieving an ecumenical consensus? His final conclusion is that there is no "moment of ordination" at all, nor that it is even adequate "to see the whole ordination prayer as that which makes someone a minister." Rather, he says,

the vital elements of a valid ordination encompass far more than just the sufficiency of a particular ritual gesture, forms of words, and intention. They extend from God's initial call of the candidate and the testing and eventual validation of that call by the church, which then appoints the ordinand to a particular ministerial charge, through the act of prayer by the people for the gifts necessary for the fruitful exercise of that ministry, of which the ordination prayer with imposition of hands forms the conclusion, to the final recognition by the people of the newly ordained's ministerial role among them, expressed in their acceptance of his or her performance of the liturgical functions belonging to that office.

All these, Bradshaw proposes, are the "vital" elements of a "valid" ordination. If so, it will then be logically asked, if any one or two or three or more of these elements are missing, is it still an ordination? And why continue to use the word "valid" to describe it, if we are eschewing medieval and scholastic terms and concepts?

And so I reach my own conclusion. There is a necessary dimension of ecumenical consensus that must be present in any acceptable proposal for the revision of ordination rites, especially in the case of *Apostolicae curae* and the Roman Church's verdict upon Anglican orders. Professor Bradshaw's essay has opened discussion on one way that the question might move forward. My response has suggested the points on which widespread consensus and convincing evidence would be necessary. For us all to see in print what his proposals might entail, I propose that the next step should be for Dr. Bradshaw, as a reputable Anglican liturgiologist of ecumenical goodwill, actually to revise the current ordination rites of the Roman Church in the light of his views as to what is "vital" or necessary and what he thinks would be likely to gain consensus from the scholars and leaders of both churches. Let the debate proceed, and let it move from abstract considerations to a specific text!

A Roman Catholic Response

Jon Nilson*

Less than a week ago, we Western Christians were celebrating the Easter Vigil. We have just been immersed once again in Jesus' Last Supper with his apostles, in his prayer that all of his followers be one, in his surrender to the will of his Father in the garden, in his arrest, his torture, his anguishing death on the cross—and then in his glorious Resurrection.

Less than a week ago, we all stood to identify and recommit ourselves as Christians by renewing our baptismal vows. We welcomed new members into our midst, those who showed themselves our brothers and sisters in faith by professing the Apostles' Creed.

So there could hardly be a better time for a conversation like this. In the Holy Week celebrations we have encountered once again the heart, core, foundation, and essence of the Christian faith. We are now examining the factors that make for a new context for the issue of Anglican orders. Yet we do so in a deeper awareness of our shared and perennial context, the faith we hold in common, albeit as Episcopalians, Roman Catholics, Lutherans, and Syrian Orthodox.

Just a century ago, Pope Leo XIII issued *Apostolicae curae* with its negative judgment on the validity of Anglican orders. This document has cast a long and very dark shadow across our relationships and conversations for one hundred years. Cardinal Willebrands was surely right to call this "the most fundamental and deeply felt issue . . ." between our two churches.

This decision of Leo was contested at the time. The archbishops of Canterbury and York replied in *Saepius officio* (1897) not only that the Anglican Communion intended to confer the priesthood instituted by Christ, but that it maintained the doctrine of the eucharist as a sacrifice. As we now know, this decision of Leo's was questionable within the Roman Catholic Church, too. The papal commissioners, Duchesne, Gasparri, de Augustinis, and Scannell, could find no good grounds for denying the validity of Anglican orders.

If the judgment of *Apostolicae curae* was questionable then, it is even more so now. Fr. John Jay Hughes, in his writings, has argued that the Reformers seemed to downplay the Eucharist as a sacrifice only because they desired to defend the uniqueness and complete sufficiency of Christ's

* Jon Nilson is Associate Professor of Theology at Loyola University Chicago and a member of ARC-USA.

122

sacrifice on the cross. Fr. Tavard has explained how Leo's view of tradition made it nearly impossible for him to reach anything but a negative judgment on Anglican orders. Fr. Bradshaw has demonstrated the fallacy of relying on the formulae of ordinals to discern ministerial intention and sacramental faith. Fr. Yarnold has reminded us that the Pontifical Council for Promoting Christian Unity—with the concurrence of the Congregation for the Doctrine of the Faith—has accepted the ARCIC clarifications on Eucharist and ministry. Fr. Hill has brought John Zizioulas's eschatological approach into our discussions as another possible way forward. Sr. Sara Butler has pointed out that we still have a lot to learn from one another in the matter of the ordination of women.

None of these papers has defended the contemporary adequacy of *Apostolicae curae's* historical reasoning or theological arguments. No one has suggested that its negative judgment must still stand today. No one has denied—and, indeed, all have suggested in their own ways—that new historical factors and theological rationales must now be taken into account in considering Anglican orders. If and when they are, they will most likely lead to a conclusion very different from Leo XIII's.

Until that time, George Tavard speaks for many of us: "It also seems undeniable that Catholic theologians who have been engaged in ecumenical dialogue with members of the Anglican Communion are now considerably embarrassed by Leo XIII's negative findings" (Tavard, 134). These same theologians are also deeply pained by their inability to receive the Eucharist with their Episcopal sisters and brothers when we gather around the Lord's table.

So what do we do now as historians, theologians, women and men of faith? The historical data are in place. The more adequate theological perspectives, such as the *koinonia* ecclesiology, have been developed. Most, if not all, of the necessary and important notions relevant to this issue of Anglican orders have been stated, sifted, restated, argued, and restated yet again by the most knowledgeable, faithful, and respected scholars.

After one hundred years, surely the time has come to speak. Vatican II's Pastoral Constitution on the Church in the Modern World says, "In order that such persons [i.e., lay theologians] may fulfill their proper function, let it be recognized that all of the faithful, clerical and lay, possess a lawful freedom of inquiry and of thought, and the freedom to express their minds humbly and courageously about those matters in which they enjoy competence" (§62). Richard McCormick observes, "Pointedly, the conciliar statement does not limit this freedom to matters where no official position exists" (McCormick, 493).

Is it not now time—after a century—to press the Vatican respectfully but insistently to reopen the issue of Anglican orders? Merely the awareness that this is "the most fundamental and deeply felt issue," as Cardinal Willebrands himself termed it, should provoke this reexamination. The longer the issue is ignored, the more cold and insensitive does the Roman Catholic Church appear to its Anglican partner. When this issue goes unattended while the reality of a new context for its discussion becomes more and more obvious, the less credible does the Roman Catholic ecumenical commitment seem to other Christians.

To reopen the question is not to prejudge the answer. As Vatican II's Constitution on Divine Revelation declared, "This tradition which comes from the apostles develops in the Church with the help of the Holy Spirit. For there is a growth in the understanding of the realities and the words which have been handed down" (§8). Is it possible that we understand sacraments and, in particular, the sacrament of orders more adequately now than Leo XIII did then? It does not dishonor his memory nor denigrate papal authority rightly understood to respond, "Yes, it is possible and likely that we do understand these more adequately now—and we must act on that fuller understanding."

Should we not also respectfully but insistently urge that absolute reordinations of former Anglicans cease immediately? From now on, any Anglican who becomes a Roman Catholic priest should be ordained conditionally. This need not be taken as a premature reversal of the judgment of *Apostolicae curae.* Rather, it would be an effort to align Church policy more closely to the recognition of Vatican II's Decree on Ecumenism that the rites of our separated Christian brothers and sisters ". . . can truly engender a life of grace. . . ." (§3).

References

McCormick, Richard. "The Gospel of life: how to read it." *The Tablet* (15/22 April 1995), 492–495.

Tavard, George. *A Review of Anglican Orders. The Problem and the Solution.* Collegeville: Liturgical Press, 1990.

Final Commentary

FRANK T. GRISWOLD*

The question of Anglican Orders has occupied a prominent place in discussions between Anglicans and Roman Catholics for the past one hundred years. In recent days, the contributions of biblical and liturgical theology have led to a reexamination of the development of the threefold pattern of bishops, priests and deacons. At the same time, a linear view of the classical form of ministry has given way to a more dynamic understanding of ministry itself, and a new appreciation of "apostolic" in relationship to "succession." These new insights have significantly altered the original question and provided, if we are willing to take them, some new, and I believe hopeful, ways of proceeding.

Some years ago I came upon Maurice Villain's biography of Abbé Paul Couturier, a French Roman Catholic priest who died in 1953 and was known as "The Apostle of Unity." Abbé Couturier's ecumenical method was built upon a foundation of prayer and sanctification: prayer understood as a deep personal and corporate opening to the Spirit of Christ in whom all things find their coherence and unity, and sanctification as the costly and exacting process of purification and transformation whereby we, and our ecclesial communities, are conformed to the mind and heart of the risen One.

As prayer draws us more deeply into the "mystery of Christ in you, the hope of glory," we undergo a process of *metanoia*—change of heart—which obliges us to examine and hand over those elements of our various traditions which reveal themselves to be impediments to the realization of Christ's own prayer "that they all may be one."

This discipline of prayer and sanctification, when taken into the life of our various churches and communities of faith, leads to a convergence rooted in Christ which is far more tenacious and resilient than the schemes of ecclesiastical joinery and compromise which have often been short-lived. At the same time, there is the constant temptation to mistake the angel of darkness for an angel of light, and to invest our various traditions with an absolute and unalterable character which comes not from the Spirit, but from our need to cling to our own self-definitions. Prayer is dangerous because it opens us to the mind of Christ which is always seeking to enlarge

---

* Frank T. Griswold is the Episcopal Bishop of Chicago and Co-chair of ARC-USA.

our limited consciousness, and render us permeable to the radical reordering of our perceptions and values.

In Eucharistic Prayer D, a prayer which appears in both the Episcopal and Roman Catholic Liturgy and is, in turn, based upon the Liturgy of St. Basil, we ask God to "reveal" the unity of the Church. Clearly, the unity of the Church already exists in the mind of God, and it is not up to us to create it. It is our task, however, to yield our various traditions to the motions of the Spirit who draws from what is Christ's and makes it known to us, not in the sense of information but in the reality of our relationships with one another. Prayer, and the process of purification which flows from it, brings us into communion with the unity which God seeks to reveal.

The papers contained in this issue of the *Anglican Theological Review* seek to establish a new context and a fresh vantage point from which to consider the question of Anglican orders. They invite us to move beyond many of the perspectives and understandings which have been part of the discussion thus far. They also present us with a unique and privileged opportunity to collaborate with God's desire to reveal the unity of the Church.

At this point, it is up to our Roman Catholic brothers and sisters to respond. It is my hope that they will do so in the light of Abbé Couturier's discipline of prayer and sanctification, a discipline which is incumbent upon all who truly seek unity in Christ.

The English Text of *Apostolicae Curae**

LEO BISHOP

Servant of the Servants of God
In Perpetual Remembrance

We have dedicated to the welfare of the noble English nation no small portion of the Apostolic care and charity by which, helped by His grace, We endeavour to fulfil the office and follow in the footsteps of *"the Great Shepherd of the sheep,"* Our Lord Jesus Christ. The Letter, which last year We sent to *the English seeking the kingdom of Christ in the unity of the faith,* is a special witness of Our good will towards England. In it We recalled the memory of the ancient union of her people with Mother Church, and We strove to hasten the day of a happy reconciliation by stirring up men's hearts to offer diligent prayer to God. And, again, more recently, when it seemed good to Us to treat more fully the Unity of the Church in a general Letter, England had not the last place in Our mind, in the hope that Our teaching might both strengthen Catholics and bring the saving light to those divided from Us.

It is pleasing to acknowledge the generous way in which Our zeal and plainness of speech, inspired by no mere human motives, have met the approval of the English people; and this testifies not less to their courtesy than to the solicitude of many for their eternal salvation.

1. Reasons for Re-opening the Question

With the same mind and intention We have now determined to turn Our consideration to a matter of no less importance, which is closely connected with the same subject and with Our desires. For already the general belief, confirmed more than once by the action and constant practice of the Church, maintained that when in England, shortly after it was rent from the centre of Christian unity, a new rite for conferring Holy Orders was publicly introduced under Edward VI., the true Sacrament of Orders, as instituted by Christ, lapsed, and with it the hierarchical succession. For some time, however, and in these last years especially, a controversy has sprung up as to whether the Sacred Orders conferred according to the Edwardine Ordinal possessed the nature and effect of a sacrament: those in favour of the

* Translation published with permission of SPCK, London.

127

absolute validity, or of a doubtful validity, being not only certain Anglican writers, but some few Catholics, chiefly non-English. The consideration of the excellency of the Christian priesthood moved Anglican writers in this matter, desirous as they were that their own people should not lack the twofold power over the Body of Christ. Catholic writers were impelled by a wish to smooth the way for the return of Anglicans to holy unity. Both, indeed, thought that in view of studies brought up to the level of recent research, and of new documents rescued from oblivion, it was not inopportune to re-examine the question by Our authority. And We, not disregarding such desires and opinions, and, above all, obeying the dictates of Apostolic charity, have considered that nothing should be left untried that might in any way tend to preserve souls from injury or procure their advantage.

2. Prescribed Method of Examination

It has, therefore, pleased Us to graciously permit the cause to be re-examined so that through the extreme care taken in the new examination all doubt, or even shadow of doubt, should be removed for the future. To this end We commissioned a certain number of men noted for their learning and ability, whose opinions in this matter were known to be divergent, to state the grounds of their judgments in writing. We then, having summoned them to Our person, directed them to interchange writings and further to investigate and discuss all that was necessary for a full knowledge of the matter. We were careful also that they should be able to re-examine all documents bearing on this question which were known to exist in the Vatican archives, to search for new ones, and even to have at their disposal all acts relating to this subject which are preserved by the Holy Office—or as it is called the *Supreme* Council—and to consider whatever had up to this time been adduced by learned men on both sides. We ordered them, when prepared in this way, to meet together in special sessions. These to the number of twelve were held under the presidency of one of the Cardinals of the Holy Roman Church, appointed by Ourselves, and all were invited to free discussion. Finally We directed that the acts of these meetings, together with all other documents, should be submitted to Our Venerable Brethren, the Cardinals of the same Council, so that when all had studied the whole subject, and discussed it in Our presence, each might give his opinion.

3. Previous Decisions, Julius III and Paul IV

This order for discussing the matter having been determined upon, it was necessary, with a view to forming a true estimate of the real state of the question, to enter upon it, after careful enquiry as to how the matter stood in relation to the prescription and settled custom of the Apostolic See, the origin and force of which custom it was undoubtedly of great importance to determine. For this reason, in the first place, the principal documents in which Our Predecessors, at the request of Queen Mary, exercised their special care for the reconciliation of the English Church, were considered. Thus Julius III. sent Cardinal Reginald Pole, an Englishman, and illustrious in many ways, to be his Legate a latere for the purpose, *"as his angel of peace and love,"* and gave him extraordinary and unusual mandates or faculties and directions for his guidance. These Paul IV. confirmed and explained. And here, to interpret rightly the force of these documents, it is necessary to lay it down as a fundamental principle that they were certainly not intended to deal with an abstract state of things, but with a specific and concrete issue. For since the faculties given by these Pontiffs to the Apostolic Legate had reference to England only, and to the state of religion therein, and since the rules of action were laid down by them at the request of the said Legate, they could not have been mere directions for determining the necessary conditions for the validity of Ordinations in general. They must pertain directly to providing for Holy Orders in the said kingdom, as the recognised condition of the circumstances and times demanded. This, besides being clear from the nature and form of the said documents, is also obvious from the fact that it would have been altogether irrelevant to thus instruct the Legate—one whose learning had been conspicuous in the Council of Trent—as to the conditions necessary for the bestowal of the Sacrament of Orders.

To all rightly estimating these matters it will not be difficult to understand why, in the Letters of Julius III., issued to the Apostolic Legate on March 8, 1554, there is a distinct mention, first of those who *"rightly and lawfully promoted"* might be maintained in their Orders; and then of others who, *"not promoted to Sacred Orders,"* might *"be promoted if they were found to be worthy and fitting subjects."* For it is clearly and definitely noted, as indeed was the case, that there were two classes of men: the first those who had really received Sacred Orders, either before the secession of Henry VIII., or, if after it and by ministers infected by error and schism, still according to the accustomed Catholic rite; the second, those who were initiated according to the Edwardine Ordinal, who on that account could be *"promoted,"* since they had received an ordination which was null. And that the mind of the Pope was this and nothing else is clearly confirmed by the Letter of the said Legate (January 29, 1555), subdelegating his faculties to the Bishop of Norwich. Moreover, what the Letters of Julius III. themselves say about freely using the Pontifical faculties, even in behalf of those who had received their consecration *"minus rite and not according to the accustomed form of the Church,"* is to be especially noted. By this expression those only could be meant who had been consecrated according to the

Edwardine rite, since besides it and the Catholic form there was then no other in England.

This becomes even still clearer when we consider the legation which, on the advice of Cardinal Pole, the Sovereign Princes, Philip and Mary, sent to the Pope in Rome in the month of February, 1555. The royal ambassadors—three men, *"most illustrious and endowed with every virtue,"* of whom one was Thomas Thirlby, Bishop of Ely—were charged to inform the Pope more fully as to the religious condition of the country, and especially to beg that he would ratify and confirm what the Legate had been at pains to effect, and had succeeded in effecting, towards the reconciliation of the kingdom with the Church. For this purpose all the necessary written evidence and the pertinent parts of the new Ordinal were submitted to the Pope. The Legation having been splendidly received, and their evidence having been *"diligently discussed"* by several of the Cardinals, *"after mature deliberation,"* Paul IV. issued his Bull *Praeclara carissimi* on June 20 of that same year. In this, whilst giving full force and approbation to what Pole had done, it is ordered in the matter of the Ordinations as follows: *"Those who have been promoted to Ecclesiastical Orders . . . by any one but by a bishop validly and lawfully ordained are bound to receive those Orders again."* But who those bishops not *"validly and lawfully ordained"* were had been made sufficiently clear by the foregoing documents and the faculties used in the said matter by the Legate: those, namely, who have been promoted to the Episcopate, as others to other Orders *"not according to the accustomed form of the Church,"* or, as the Legate himself wrote to the Bishop of Norwich, *"the form and intention of the Church"* not having been observed. These were certainly those promoted according to the new form of rite, to the examination of which the Cardinals specially deputed had given their careful attention. Neither should the passage much to the point in the same Pontifical Letter be overlooked where, together with others needing dispensation, are enumerated those *"who had obtained as well orders as benefices nulliter et de facto."* For to obtain orders *nulliter* means the same as by an act null and void, that is *invalid,* as the very meaning of the word and as common parlance require. This is especially clear when the word is used in the same way about orders as about *"ecclesiastical benefices."* These, by the undoubted teaching of the sacred canons, were clearly null if given with any vitiating defect. Moreover, when some doubted as to who, according to the mind of the Pontiff, could be called and considered bishops *"validly and lawfully ordained,"* the said Pope shortly after, on October 30, issued further Letters in the form of a Brief, and said: *"We, wishing to remove the doubt and to opportunely provide for the peace of conscience of those who during the schism were promoted to Orders, by expressing more clearly the mind and intention which We had in the aforesaid Letters, declare that only those Bishops and Archbishops, who were not ordained and consecrated in the form of the Church cannot be said to have been validly and lawfully ordained.*" Unless this declaration had applied to the actual case in England, that is to say to the Edwardine Ordinal, the Pope would certainly have done nothing by these last Letters for the removal of doubt and the restoration of peace of conscience. Further, it was in this sense that the Legate understood the documents and commands of the Apostolic See and duly and conscientiously obeyed them; and the same was done by Queen Mary and the rest who helped to restore Catholicism to its former state.

4. Invariable Practice of the Holy See

The authority of Julius III. and of Paul IV., which we have quoted, clearly shows the origin of that practice which has been observed without interruption for more than three centuries, that Ordinations conferred according to the Edwardine rite should be considered null and void. This practice is fully proved by the numerous cases of absolute re-ordination according to the Catholic rite even in Rome. In the observance of this practice we have a proof directly affecting the matter in hand. For if by any chance doubt should remain as to the true sense in which these Pontifical documents are to be understood, the principle holds good that *"Custom is the best interpreter of law."* Since in the Church it has ever been a constant and established rule that it is sacrilegious to repeat the Sacrament of Order, it never could have come to pass that the Apostolic See should have silently acquiesced in and tolerated such a custom. But not only did the Apostolic See tolerate this practice, but approved and sanctioned it as often as any particular case arose which called for its judgment in the matter. We adduce two facts of this kind out of many which have from time to time been submitted to the Supreme Council of the Holy Office. The first was (in 1684) of a certain French Calvinist, and the other (in 1704) of John Clement Gordon; both of whom had received their Orders according to the Edwardine ritual. In the first case, after a searching investigation, the consultors, not a few in number, gave in writing their answers—or, as they call it, their *vota*—and the rest unanimously agreed with their conclusion, *"for the invalidity of the Ordination,"* and only on account of reasons of opportuneness did the Cardinals deem it well to answer by a *"dilata"* [viz. not to formulate the conclusion at the moment]. The same documents were called into use and considered again in the examination of the second case, and additional written statements of opinion were also obtained from consultors, and the most eminent doctors of the Sorbonne and of Douai were likewise asked for their opinion. No safeguard, which wisdom and prudence could suggest to ensure the thorough sifting of the question, was neglected.

5. Decree of Clement XI and Its Importance

And here it is important to observe that although Gordon himself, whose case it was, and some of the consultors had adduced, amongst the reasons which went to prove the invalidity, the Ordination of Parker, according to their own ideas about it, in the delivery of the decision this reason was altogether set aside, as documents of incontestable authenticity prove. Nor, in pronouncing the decision, was weight given to any other reason than the *"defect of form and intention"*; and in order that the judgment concerning this form might be more certain and complete, precaution was taken that a copy of the Anglican Ordinal should be submitted to examination, and that with it should be collated the Ordination forms gathered together from the various Eastern and Western rites. Then Clement XI. himself, with the unanimous vote of the Cardinals concerned, on the *"Feria V.,"* April 17, 1704, *decreed:* "John Clement Gordon shall be ordained from *the beginning and unconditionally* to all the Orders, even Sacred Orders, and chiefly of priesthood, and in case he has not been confirmed, he shall first receive the Sacrament of Confirmation." It is important to bear in mind that this judgment was in no wise determined by the omission of the *tradition of instruments,* for in such a case, according to the established custom, the direction would have been to repeat the Ordination *conditionally;* and still more important it is to note that the judgment of the Pontiff applies universally to all Anglican Ordinations, because, although it refers to a particular case, it is not based upon any reason special to that case, but upon the defect of form, which defect equally affects all these Ordinations: so much so, that when similar cases subsequently came up for decision the same decree of Clement XI. was quoted as the norma.

6. The Question already Definitely Settled

Hence it must be clear to everyone that the controversy lately revived had been already definitely settled by the Apostolic See, and that it is to the insufficient knowledge of these documents that We must perhaps attribute the fact that any Catholic writer should have considered it still an open question. But, as We stated at the beginning, there is nothing We so deeply and ardently desire as to be of help to men of good will by showing them the greatest consideration and charity. Wherefore We ordered that the Anglican Ordinal, which is the essential point of the whole matter, should be once more most carefully examined.

7. The Anglican Ordinal

In the examination of any rite for the effecting and administering of Sacrament, distinction is rightly made between the part which is *ceremonial* and that which is *essential,* usually called the *matter and form.* All know that the Sacraments of the New Law, as sensible and efficient signs of invisible grace, ought both to signify the grace which they effect, and effect the grace which they signify. Although the signification ought to be found in the whole essential rite—that is to say, in the matter and form—it still pertains chiefly to the form; since the matter is the part which is not determined by itself, but which is determined by the form. And this appears still more clearly in the Sacrament of Orders, the matter of which, in so far as We have to consider it in this case, is the imposition of hands, which indeed by itself signifies nothing definite, and is equally used for several Orders and for Confirmation. But the words which until recently were commonly held by Anglicans to constitute the proper form of priestly Ordination—namely, *"Receive the Holy Ghost,"* certainly do not in the least definitely express the Sacred Order of Priesthood, or its grace and power, which is chiefly the power *"of consecrating and of offering the true body and blood of the Lord"* (Council of Trent, Sess. XXIII., *de Sacr. Ord.,* Can. 1) in that sacrifice which is no *"nude commemoration of the sacrifice offered on the Cross"* (*Ibid.* Sess. XXII., *de Sacrif. Missae. Can. 3*). This form had indeed afterwards added to it the words *"for the office and work of a priest,"* etc.; but this rather shows that the Anglicans themselves perceived that the first form was defective and inadequate. But even if this addition could give to the form its due signification, it was introduced too late, as a century had already elapsed since the adoption of the Edwardine Ordinal, for, as the Hierarchy had become extinct, there remained no power of ordaining. In vain has help been recently sought for the plea of the validity of Orders from the other prayers of the same Ordinal. For, to put aside other reasons which show these to be insufficient for the purpose in the Anglican rite, let this argument suffice for all: from them has been deliberately removed whatever sets forth the dignity and office of the priesthood in the Catholic rite. That form consequently cannot be considered apt or sufficient for the Sacrament which omits what it ought essentially to signify.

The same holds good of Episcopal Consecration. For to the formula *"Receive the Holy Ghost,"* not only were the words *"for the office and work of a bishop,"* etc., added at a later period, but even these, as we shall presently state, must be understood in a sense different to that which they bear in the Catholic rite. Nor is anything gained by quoting the prayer of the preface *"Almighty God,"* since it in like manner has been stripped of the words which denote the *summum sacerdotium.* It is not here relevant to examine whether the Episcopate be a completion of the priesthood or an Order distinct from it, or whether when bestowed, as they say *per saltum,* on one who is not a priest, it has or has not its effect. But the Episcopate undoubtedly by the institution of Christ most truly belongs to the Sacrament of Orders and constitutes the sacerdotium in the highest degree, namely, that which by the teaching of the Holy Fathers and our liturgical customs is called the *"summum sacerdotium, sacri ministerii summa."* So it comes to pass that, as the Sacrament of Orders, and the true sacerdotium of Christ were utterly eliminated from the Anglican rite, and hence the sacerdotium is in no wise conferred truly and validly in the Episcopal consecration of the same rite, for the like reason, therefore, the Episcopate can in no wise be truly and validly conferred by it; and this the more so because among the first duties of the Episcopate is that of ordaining ministers for the Holy Eucharist and sacrifice.

8. The Mind and Aim of those who compose the Anglican Ordinal

For the full and accurate understanding of the Anglican Ordinal, besides what we have noted as to some of its parts, there is nothing more pertinent than to consider carefully the circumstances under which it was composed and publicly authorised. It would be tedious to enter into details, nor is it necessary to do so, as the history of that time is sufficiently eloquent as to the animus of the authors of the Ordinal against the Catholic Church, as to the abettors whom they associated with themselves from the heterodox sects, and as to the end they had in view. Being fully cognisant of the necessary connection between faith and worship, between *"the law of believing and the law of praying,"* under a pretext of returning to the primitive form, they corrupted the liturgical order in many ways to suit the errors of the reformers. For this reason in the whole Ordinal not only is there no clear mention of the sacrifice, of consecration, of the sacerdotium, and of the power of consecrating and offering sacrifice, but, as we have just stated, every trace of these things, which had been in such prayers of the Catholic rite as they had not entirely rejected, was deliberately removed and struck out. In this way the native character—or spirit as it is called—of the Ordinal clearly manifests itself. Hence if vitiated in its origin, it was wholly insufficient to confer Orders, it was impossible that in the course of time it could become sufficient since no change had taken place. In vain those who, from the time of Charles I., have attempted to hold some kind of sacrifice or of priesthood, have made some additions to the Ordinal. In vain also has been the contention of that small section of the Anglican body formed in recent times, that the said Ordinal can be understood and interpreted in a sound and orthodox sense. Such efforts, We affirm, have been and are made in vain, and for this reason, that any words in the Anglican Ordinal, as it now is, which lend themselves to ambiguity, cannot be taken in the same sense as they possess in the Catholic rite. For once a new rite has been initiated in which, as we have seen, the Sacrament of Orders is adulterated or denied, and from which all idea of consecration and sacrifice has been rejected, the formula *"Receive the Holy Ghost,"* no longer holds good; because the Spirit is infused into the soul with the grace of the Sacrament, and the words, *"for the office and work of a priest or bishop,"* and the like no longer hold good, but remain as words without the reality which Christ instituted.

Several of the more shrewd Anglican interpreters of the Ordinal have perceived the force of this argument, and they openly urge it against those who take the Ordinal in a new sense and vainly attach to the Orders conferred thereby a value and efficacy which they do not possess. By this same argument is refuted the contention of those who think that the prayer *"Almighty God giver of all good things,"* which is found at the beginning of the ritual action, might suffice as a legitimate form of Orders, even in the hypothesis that it might be held to be sufficient in a Catholic rite approved by the Church.

9. Catholic Doctrine of Intention

With this inherent *defect of form* is joined the *defect of intention,* which is equally essential to the Sacrament. The Church does not judge about the mind or intention in so far as it is something by its nature internal; but in so far as it is manifested externally she is bound to judge concerning it. When anyone has rightly and seriously made use of the due form and the matter requisite for effecting or conferring the Sacrament he is considered by the very fact to do what the Church does. On this principle rests the doctrine that a Sacrament is truly conferred by the ministry of one who is a heretic or unbaptised, provided the Catholic rite be employed. On the other hand if the rite be changed, with the manifest intention of introducing another rite not approved by the Church and of rejecting what the Church does, and what by the institution of Christ belongs to the nature of the Sacrament, then it is clear that not only is the necessary intention wanting to the Sacrament, but that the intention is adverse to and destructive of the Sacrament.

10. Decision of the Holy Office and the Pope's Final Decree

All these matters have been long and carefully considered by Ourselves and by Our Venerable Brethren, the Judges of the Supreme Council, of whom it has pleased Us to call a special meeting upon the *"Feria V.,"* the

16th day of July last, upon the solemnity of our Lady of Mount Carmel. They with one accord agreed that the question laid before them had been already adjudicated upon with full knowledge of the Apostolic See, and that this renewed discussion and examination of the issues had only served to bring out more clearly the wisdom and accuracy with which that decision had been made. Nevertheless We deemed it well to postpone a decision in order to afford time, both to consider whether it would be fitting or expedient that We should make a fresh authoritative declaration upon the matter, and to humbly pray for a fuller measure of Divine guidance. Then, considering that this matter of practice, although already decided had been by certain persons, for whatever reason, recalled into discussion, and that thence it might follow that a pernicious error would be fostered in the minds of many who might suppose that they possessed the Sacrament and effects of Orders, where these are nowise to be found it has seemed good to Us in the Lord to pronounce Our judgment.

Wherefore, strictly adhering in this matter to the decrees of the Pontiffs, Our Predecessors, and confirming them most fully, and, as it were, renewing them by Our Authority, of Our own motion and certain knowledge We pronounce and declare that Ordinations carried out according to the Anglican rite have been and are absolutely null and utterly void.

It remains for Us to say that even as We have entered upon the elucidation of this grave question in the name and in the love of the *Great Shepherd* in the Same We appeal to those who desire and seek with a sincere heart the possession of a hierarchy and of Orders. Perhaps until now aiming at the greater perfection of Christian virtue, and searching more devoutly the Divine Scriptures and redoubling the fervour of their prayers, they have, nevertheless, hesitated in doubt and anxiety to follow the voice of Christ, which so long has interiorly admonished them. Now they see clearly whither He in His goodness invites them and wills them to come. In returning to His one only fold, they will obtain the blessings which they seek, and the consequent helps to salvation of which He has made the Church, the dispenser, and, as it were, the constant guardian and promoter of His Redemption amongst the nations. Then indeed *"they shall draw waters in joy from the fountains of the Saviour,"* His wondrous Sacraments, whereby His faithful souls have their sins truly remitted, and are restored to the friendship of God, and nourished and strengthened by the Heavenly Bread, and abound with the most powerful aids for their eternal salvation. May the God of Peace, the God of all consolation, in His infinite tenderness enrich and fill with all these blessings those who truly yearn for them. We wish to direct Our exhortation and Our desires in a special way to those who are ministers of religion in their respective communities. They are men who from their very office take precedence in learning and authority, and who have at heart the glory of God and the salvation of souls. Let them be the first in joyfully submitting to the Divine call, and obey it and furnish a glorious example to others. Assuredly with an exceeding great joy their Mother, the Church, will welcome them and will cherish with all her love and care those whom the strength of their generous souls has amidst many trials and difficulties led back to her bosom. Nor could words express the recognition which this devoted courage will win for them from the assemblies of the brethren throughout the Catholic world, or what hope or confidence it will merit for them before Christ as their Judge, or what reward it will obtain from Him in the Heavenly Kingdom! And We ourselves in every lawful way shall continue to promote their reconciliation with the Church in which individuals and masses, as We ardently desire, may find so much for their imitation. In the meantime, by the tender mercy of the Lord Our God, We ask and beseech all to strive faithfully to follow in the open path of Divine Grace and Truth.

We decree that these Letters and all things contained therein shall not be liable at any time to be impugned or objected to by reason of fault or any other defect whatsoever of subreption or obreption or of Our intention, but are and shall be always valid and in force, and shall be inviolably observed both juridically and otherwise, by all of whatsoever degree and pre-eminence; declaring null and void anything which in these matters may happen to be contrariwise attempted, whether wittingly or unwittingly, by any person whatsoever by, whatsoever authority or pretext, all things to the contrary notwithstanding.

The English Text of *Saepius Officio**

(Edited excerpts)

ANSWER OF THE ARCHBISHOPS OF ENGLAND TO THE APOSTOLIC LETTER OF POPE LEO XIII. ON ENGLISH ORDINATIONS

Addressed to the whole body of Bishops of the Catholic Church

1. It is the fortune of our office that often, when we would fain write about the common salvation, an occasion arises for debating some controverted question which cannot be postponed to another time. This certainly was recently the case when in the month of September last there suddenly arrived in this country from Rome a letter, already printed and published, which aimed at overthrowing our whole position as a Church. It was upon this letter that our minds were engaged with the attention it demanded when our beloved brother Edward, at that time Archbishop of Canterbury, Primate of all England and Metropolitan, was in God's providence taken from us by sudden death. In his last written words he bequeathed to us the treatment of the question which he was doubtless himself about to treat with the greatest learning and theological grace. It has therefore seemed good to us, the Archbishops and Primates of England, that this answer should be written in order that the truth on this matter might be made known both to our venerable brother Pope Leo XIIIth, in whose name the letter from Rome was issued, and also to all the other bishops of the Christian Church settled throughout the world.

II. The duty indeed is a serious one; one which cannot be discharged without a certain deep and strong emotion. But since we firmly believe that we have been truly ordained by the Chief Shepherd to bear a part of His tremendous office in the Catholic Church, we are not at all disturbed by the opinion expressed in that letter. So we approach the task which is of necessity laid upon us "in the spirit of meekness"; and we deem it of greater importance to make plain for all time our doctrine about holy orders and other matters pertaining to them, than to win a victory in controversy over a sister Church of Christ. Still it is necessary that our answer be cast in a

---

* Translation published with permission of SPCK, London.

controversial form lest it be said by anyone that we have shrunk from the force of the arguments put forward on the other side.

III.. . . . There has been a more recent and a more bitter controversy on the validity of Anglican ordinations, into which theologians on the Roman side have thrown themselves with eagerness, and in doing so have, for the most part, imputed to us various crimes and defects. There are others, and those not the least wise among them, who, with a nobler feeling, have undertaken our defence. But no decision of the Roman pontiffs, fully supported by arguments, has ever before appeared, nor has it been possible for us, while we knew that the practice of reordaining our Priests clearly prevailed (though this practice has not been without exception), to learn on what grounds of defect they were reordained. We knew of the unworthy struggles about Formosus, and the long vacillations about heretical, schismatic and simoniacal ordinations. We had access to the letter of Innocent IIId on the necessity of supplying unction and the Decree of Eugenius IVth for the Armenians; we had the historical documents of the XVIth century, though of these many are unknown even to the present day; we had various decisions of later Popes, Clement XIth and Benedict XIVth, but those of Clement were couched in general terms and therefore uncertain. We had also the Roman Pontifical as reformed from time to time, but, as it now exists, so confusedly arranged as to puzzle rather than enlighten the minds of enquirers. For if any one considers the rite *Of the ordination of a Presbyter,* he sees that the proper laying on of hands stands apart from the utterance of the form. He also cannot tell whether the man, who in the rubrics is called "ordained," has really been ordained, or whether the power, which is given at the end of the office by the words—"Receive the Holy Ghost; whose sins thou shalt have remitted they are remitted unto them, and whose sins thou shalt have retained they are retained"—with the laying on of pontifical hands, is a necessary part of the priesthood (as the Council of Trent seems to teach) or not necessary. In like manner if anyone reads through the rite *Of the consecration of an elect as Bishop,* he will nowhere find that he is called "Bishop" in the prayers and benedictions referring to the man to be consecrated, or that "Episcopate" is spoken of in them in regard to him. As far as the prayers are concerned the term "Episcopate" occurs for the first time in the Mass during the consecration.

From these documents therefore, so obviously discordant and indefinite, no one, however wise, could extract with certainty what was considered by the Roman Pontiffs to be truly essential and necessary to holy orders.

IV. Thus our most venerable brother in his letter dated the 13th of September, which begins with the words *Apostolicae curae,* has approached this question after a manner hitherto unexampled, although the arguments urged by him are sufficiently old. Nor do we desire to deny that in entering upon this controversy he has consulted the interests of the Church and of truth in throwing over the very vain opinion about the necessity of the delivery of the "instruments," which was nevertheless widely accepted by scholastic theologians from the time of S. Thomas Aquinas up to that of Benedict XIVth, and even up to the present day. At the same time he has done well in neglecting other errors and fallacies, which for our part also we shall neglect in this reply, and in regard to which we hope that theologians on the Roman side will follow his example and neglect them for the future.

V. His whole judgment therefore hinges on two points, namely, on the practice of the Court of Rome and the form of the Anglican rite, to which is attached a third question, not easy to separate from the second, on the intention of our Church. We will answer at once about the former, though it is, in our opinion, of less importance.

VI. As regards the practice of the Roman Court and Legate in the XVIth century, although the Pope writes at some length, we believe that he is really as uncertain as ourselves. We see that he has nothing to add to the documents which are already well known, and that he quotes and argues from an imperfect copy of the letter of Paul IVth *Praeclara carissimi*. Where, for example, are the faculties granted to Pole after 5 August 1553 and before 8 March 1554, which Julius confirms in his letter of the latter date, to be "freely used" in respect to orders received with any irregularity or failure in the accustomed form, but does not detail and define? Without these faculties the "rules of action" to be observed by Pole are imperfectly known. For the distinction made in the letters of both those dates between men "promoted" and "not promoted," to which the Pope refers, does not seem to touch the position of the Edwardian clergy, but the case of those who held benefices without any pretence of ordination, as was then often done. Who in fact knows thoroughly either what was done in this matter or on what grounds it was done? We know part; of part we are ignorant. It can be proved however on our side that the work of that reconciliation under Queen Mary (6 July 1553 to 17 Nov. 1558) was in very great measure finished, under royal and episcopal authority, before the arrival of Pole.

In the conduct of which business there is evidence of much inconsistency and unevenness. Yet while many Edwardian Priests are found to have been deprived for various reasons, and particularly on account of entering into wedlock, none are so found, as far as we know, on account of defect of Order. Some were voluntarily reordained. Some received anointing as a supplement to their previous ordination, a ceremony to which some of our Bishops at that time attached great importance. Some, and perhaps the majority, remained in their benefices without reordination, nay were promoted in some cases to new cures. Pole did not return to England after his exile until November 1554, and brought the reconciliation to a conclusion in the fifteen months that followed. The principle of his work appears to have been to recognise the state of things which he found in existence on his

arrival, and to direct all his powers towards the restoration of papal supremacy as easily as possible. In this period one man and perhaps a second (for
more have not yet been discovered) received new orders under Pole, in the
years 1554 and 1557; but it is uncertain in what year each of them began the
process of being reordained. At any rate very few were reordained after
Pole's arrival. Others perhaps received some kind of supplement or other to
their orders, a record of which is not to be found in our Registers.

But if a large number had been reordained under Pole, as papal legate,
it would not have been at all surprising, inasmuch as in his twelve legatine
constitutions, he added, as an appendix to the second, the Decree of Eugenius IVth for the Armenians, saying that he did so "inasmuch as very great
errors have been committed here (in England) with respect to the doctrine
concerning the head of the Church and the Sacraments." And this he did,
not as our Archbishop, but as papal legate. For these constitutions were
promulgated at the beginning of the year 1556. But Pole was only ordained
Presbyter on the 20th March of the same year; and said Mass for the first
time on the following day, being the day on which our lawful Archbishop,
Cranmer, was burnt alive; and on the 22nd he was consecrated Archbishop.

We quote here the Decree of Eugenius IVth, as reissued by Pole,
because it shows how slippery and weak the judgment of the Church of
Rome has been in this matter. Further when Pope Leo extols the learning
of Pole on this point and writes that it would have been quite irrelevant for
the Popes to instruct the legate "as to the conditions necessary for the
bestowal of the sacrament of orders," he seems wholly to forget Eugenius'
Decree, which he has silently thrown over in another part of his letter. (Cp.
part 3 and part 5.). . . . Now in our Church from March 1550 to 1st
November 1552, though the delivery of the instruments still remained in
some degree (i.e., of the chalice with bread in the case of Presbyters, and of
the pastoral staff in that of Bishops, and of the Bible in both) yet the forms
attached to them had already been changed very nearly into those which
now are in use. In the year 1552 the delivery of the chalice and the staff was
dropped and that of the Bible alone remained. King Edward died on the 6th
July 1553.

According to this Decree, then, all these Presbyters ought to have been
reordained. But Pole's opinion scarcely agreed with his practice. Nor does
Paul IVth himself, in his Brief *Regimini universalis,* make any demands as
to the form in which Presbyters are ordained, though careful about "properly and rightly ordained" Bishops. . . .

VIII. The Pope has certainly done well not to rest satisfied with such
weak conclusions, and to determine to reopen the question and to treat it
afresh; although this would seem to have been done in appearance rather
than in reality. For inasmuch as the case was submitted by him to the holy
Office, it is clear that it, being bound by its traditions, could hardly have

expressed dissent from the judgment, however ill founded, which was passed in the case of Gordon.

Further when he touches upon the matter itself and follows the steps of the Council of Trent, our opinion does not greatly differ from the main basis of his judgment. He rightly calls laying on of hands the "matter" of ordination. His judgment on the "form" is not so clearly expressed; but we suppose him to intend to say that the form is prayer or benediction appropriate to the ministry to be conferred, which is also our opinion. Nor do we part company with the Pope when he suggests that it is right to investigate the intention of a Church in conferring holy orders "in so far as it is manifested externally." For whereas it is scarcely possible for any man to arrive at a knowledge of the inner mind of a Priest, so that it cannot be right to make the validity of a Sacrament depend upon it, the will of the Church can both be ascertained more easily, and ought also to be both true and sufficient. Which intention our Church shows generally by requiring a promise from one who is to be ordained that he will rightly minister the Doctrine, Sacraments and Discipline of Christ, and teaches that he who is unfaithful to this promise, may be justly punished. And in our Liturgy we regularly pray for "all Bishops and Curates, that they may both by their life and doctrine set forth (God's) true and lively word, and rightly and duly administer (His) holy Sacraments."

But the intention of the Church must be ascertained "in so far as it is manifested externally," that is to say, from its public formularies and definite pronouncements which directly touch the main point of the question, not from its omissions and reforms, made as opportunity occurs, in accordance with the liberty which belongs to every Province and Nation—unless it may be that something is omitted which has been ordered in the Word of God, or the known and certain statutes of the universal Church. For if a man assumes the custom of the middle ages and of more recent centuries as the standard, consider, brethren, how clearly he is acting against the liberty of the Gospel and the true character of Christendom. And if we follow this method of judging the validity of Sacraments, we must throw doubt upon all of them, except Baptism alone, which seems according to the judgment of the universal Church to have its matter and form ordained by the Lord.

IX. We acknowledge therefore with the Pope that laying on of hands is the matter of ordination; we acknowledge that the form is prayer or blessing appropriate to the ministry to be conferred; we acknowledge that the intention of the Church, as far as it is externally manifested, is to be ascertained, so that we may discover if it agrees with the mind of the Lord and His Apostles and with the Statutes of the Universal Church. We do not however attach so much weight to the doctrine so often descanted upon by the Schoolmen since the time of William of Auxerre (A.D. 1215), that each of the Sacraments of the Church ought to have a single form and matter exactly defined. Nor do we suppose that this is a matter of faith with the Romans. For it introduces a very great danger of error, supposing any Pope or Doctor, who may have great influence over the men of his own time, should persuade people to acknowledge as necessary this or that form or matter which has not been defined either in the word of God or by the Catholic Fathers or Councils.

For, as we have said, Baptism stands alone as a Sacrament in being quite certain both in its form and its matter. And this is suitable to the nature of the case. For,—inasmuch as the Baptism of Christ is the entrance into the Church for all men, and can be ministered by all Christians, if there be a pressing need,—the conditions of a valid Baptism ought to be known to all. As regards the Eucharist (if you set aside, as of less importance, questions about unleavened bread, and salt, about water, and the rest), it has a sufficiently certain matter: but up to the present day a debate is still going on as to its full and essential form. But the matter of Confirmation is not so entirely certain; and we at any rate do not at all think that Christians who have different opinions on the subject should be condemned by one an-other. The form of Confirmation again is uncertain and quite general, prayer, that is to say, or benediction, more or less suitable, such as is used in each of our Churches. And so with respect to others. . . .

XII. What therefore is the reason for impugning our form and intention in ordaining Presbyters and Bishops?

The Pope writes, if we omit things of less importance, "that the order of priesthood or its grace and power, which is especially the power *of consecrating and offering the true Body and Blood of the Lord* in that sacrifice which is *no nude commemoration of the sacrifice* offered on the cross" must be expressed in the ordering of a Presbyter. What he desires in the form of consecration of a Bishop is not so clear; but it seems that, in his opinion, in some way or other, "high priesthood" ought to be attributed to him.

Both however of these opinions are strange, inasmuch as in the most ancient Roman formulary used, as it seems, at the beginning of the third century after Christ (seeing that exactly the same form is employed both for a Bishop and a Presbyter, except the name), nothing whatever is said about "high priesthood" or "priesthood" nor about the sacrifice of the Body and Blood of Christ. "The prayers and oblations which he will offer (to God) by day and by night" are alone mentioned, and the power of remitting sins is touched on. . . .

XIII. On the subject of the title of Bishops our simple and immediate reply is that the name of high Priest is in no way necessary to describe this office in the form of consecration. The African Church openly forbad even her Primates to use this title, the words "pontifical glory," which sometimes appear in Sacramentaries, denote a secular or Jewish distinction rather than a rank in the Church. We are content with the name of Bishop to describe the office of those who, when they were left, after the removal of the Apostles, to be chief pastors in the Church, exercised the right of ordaining and confirming, and ruled, together with a body of presbyters, over a single "parochia" or diocese, as it is now called. And to this order the Pope, in the beginning of his letter, following the sound custom of antiquity, reckons himself to belong. Bishops are undoubtedly Priests, just as Presbyters are Priests, and in early ages they enjoyed this title more largely than Presbyters did; nay, it was not till the fourth or fifth century that Presbyters, in the Latin Church at any rate, came to be called Priests in their own right. But it does not therefore follow that Bishops nowadays ought to be called high Priests in the form of Consecration. The question of the priesthood of Bishops was perhaps different in early times, certainly up to the IXth and possibly to the XIth century, when a simple Deacon was often made Bishop *per saltum,* i.e. without passing through the presbyterate. In those days of course it was fitting, if not indeed necessary, to apply to the Bishop the term Priest, as, e.g. is done in the Prayer still used in the Pontifical, which speaks of "the horn of priestly grace." But inasmuch as this custom of consecration *per saltum* has long since died out (though perhaps never expressly forbidden by statute) and every Bishop has already, during the period of his presbyterate, been a Priest, it is no longer necessary to confer the priesthood afresh, nor, if we give our candid opinion, is it a particularly good and regular proceeding. Nor ought the Romans to require it, inasmuch as the Council of Trent calls preaching of the Gospel "the chief duty of Bishops." It is not therefore necessary that either high priesthood or any other fresh priesthood should be attributed to Bishops.

But although in our Ordinal we say nothing about high Priests and Pontiffs, we do not avoid using the terms in other public documents. Examples may be taken from the Latin edition of the *Book of Common Prayer,* A.D. 1560, from the letter written by twelve Bishops on behalf of Archbishop Grindall, A.D. 1580, and from Archbishop Whitgift's Commission to his Suffragan the Bishop of Dover, A.D. 1583. . . .

XVII. Now the intention of our Church, not merely of a newly formed party in it, is quite clearly set forth in the title and preface of the Ordinal. The title in 1552 ran "The fourme and manner of makynge and consecratynge Bishoppes, Priestes and Deacons." The preface immediately following begins thus:—"It is euident unto all men, diligently readinge holye Scripture and auncient aucthours, that from the Apostles tyme there hathe bene these ordres of Ministers in Christ's Church: Bishoppes, Priestes, and Deacons: which Offices were euermore had in suche reuerent estimacion, that no man by his own private aucthoritie might presume to execute any of them, except he were first called, tried, examined, and knowen to have such qualities as were requisite for the same; And also, by publique prayer, with imposicion of hands, approued, and admitted thereunto. And therfore, to the entent that these orders shoulde bee continued, and reuerentlye used and estemed, in this Church of England; it is requysite that no man (not beyng at thys presente Bisshope, Priest nor Deacon) shall execute anye of them, excepte he be called, tryed, examined and admitted, accordynge to the form hereafter folowinge." Further on it is stated incidentally that "euery man which is to be consecrated a Bishop shalbe fully thyrtie yeres of age." And in the rite itself the "consecration" of the Bishop is repeatedly mentioned. The succession and continuance of these offices from the Lord through the Apostles and the other ministers of the primitive Church is also clearly implied in the "Eucharistical" prayers which precede the words *Receive the Holy Ghost.* Thus the intention of our Fathers was to keep and continue these offices which come down from the earliest times, and "reverently to use and esteem them," in the sense, of course, in which they were received from the Apostles and had been up to that time in use. This is a point on which the Pope is unduly silent.

XVIII. But all this and other things of the same kind are called by Pope Leo "names without the reality instituted by Christ." But, on the contrary, our Fathers' fundamental principle was to refer everything to the authority of the Lord, revealed in the Holy Scriptures. It was for this that they rescinded ceremonies composed and added by men, even including that best known one, common to the modern Latin and Eastern churches, though unknown to the ancient Roman church, of holding a copy of the Gospels over the head of one about to be ordained Bishop during the utterance of the blessing and the laying on of hands.

Thus then our Fathers employed one matter in imprinting the character, viz., the laying on of hands, one matter in the commission to minister publicly and exercise powers over the flock entrusted to each, viz., the delivery of the Bible or Gospels. This last they probably borrowed from the office of inaugurating a new Bishop and similar rites; thus in the Pontifical the Gospels are still delivered to the Bishop after the ring is given. Other ceremonies of somewhat later date and imported into the ancient Roman Ordinal from sources for the most part foreign and especially Gallican, such as the delivery of the instruments and ornaments, the blessing and unction of hands and head, with the accompanying prayers, they cut out as they had a full right to do. The porrection of the instruments came, as is well known, from the formularies of minor orders and was unknown to any Pontifical before the XIth century, which appears to be the earliest date of its mention in writing. When it was reformed, the new formula "Receive the power of offering sacrifice to God and of celebrating mass (or, as in the Roman Pontifical, masses) on behalf of both the quick and dead" was likewise dropped. The prayer for the blessing of the hands could be said or omitted at the discretion of the Bishop even before the XVIth century. The anointing is a Gallican and British custom, not Roman at all. . . .

XIX. What wonder then if our Fathers, wishing to return to the simplicity of the Gospel, eliminated these prayers from a liturgy which was to be read publicly in a modern language? And herein they followed a course which was certainly opposed to that pursued by the Romans. For the Romans, starting from an almost Gospel simplicity, have relieved the austerity of their rites with Gallican embellishments, and have gradually, as time went on, added ceremonies borrowed from the Old Testament in order to emphasise the distinction between people and Priests more and more. That these ceremonies are "contemptible and harmful," or that they are useless at their proper place and time, we do by no means assert—we declare only that they are not necessary. Thus in the XVIth century when our Fathers drew up a liturgy at once for the use of the people and the clergy they went back almost to the Roman starting-point. For both sides alike, their holy Fathers, and ours, whom they call innovators, followed the same most sure leaders, the Lord and His Apostles. Now however, the example of the modern Church of Rome, which is entirely taken up with the offering of sacrifice, is held up to us as the only model for our imitation. And this is done so eagerly by the Pope that he does not hesitate to write that "whatever sets forth the dignity and offices of the priesthood" has been "deliberately removed" from the prayers of our Ordinal.

But we confidently assert that our Ordinal, particularly in this last point, is superior to the Roman Pontifical in various ways, inasmuch as it expresses more clearly and faithfully those things which by Christ's institution belong to the nature of the priesthood (part 9) and the effect of the Catholic rites used in the Universal Church. And this, in our opinion, can be shown by a comparison of the Pontifical with the Ordinal.

The Roman formulary begins with a presentation made by the Archdeacon and a double address from the Bishop, first to the clergy and people, and then to the candidates for ordination—for there is no public examination in the ordination of a presbyter. Then follows the laying-on of the Bishop's hands, and then those of the assistant presbyters, performed without any words; in regard to which obscure rite we have quoted the opinion of Cardinal de Lugo (chap. XV.). Then the three ancient prayers are said, the two short collects, and the longer Benediction (chap. XII.) which is now said by the Bishop "with his hands extended in front of his breast." This prayer, which is called the "Consecration" in ancient books, is considered by weighty authorities, since the time of Morinus, to be the true "form" of Roman ordination, and doubtless was in old days joined with laying on of hands. Now however "extension of hands" is substituted for laying on of hands, as is the case in Confirmation (chap. X.), while even that gesture is not considered necessary. At any rate, if the old Roman ordinations are valid, directly this prayer has been said the ordination of presbyters is complete in that church even at the present day. For any "form" which has once sufficed for any Sacrament of the Church, and is retained still unaltered and complete, must be supposed to be retained with the same intent as before; nor can it be asserted without a sort of sacrilege that it has lost its virtue, because other things have been silently added after it. In any case the intention of the more recent part of the Roman formulary cannot have been to empty the more ancient part of its proper force; but its object may not improperly be supposed to have been as follows, first that the priests already ordained should be prepared by various rites and ceremonies for the offering of the sacrifice, secondly that they should receive the power to offer it in explicit terms, thirdly that they should begin to exercise the right of the priesthood in the celebration of the Mass, lastly that they should be publicly invested with another priestly power, that of remitting sins. Which opinion is confirmed by the language of the old Pontificals, as for example in the Sarum Pontifical we read "Bless and sanctify these hands *of thy priests.*" All therefore that follows after that ancient "form," just like our words added in 1662, is simply not necessary. For those powers above specified can be conveyed either implicitly and by usage, as was the method in ancient times, or at once and explicitly; but the method of conveyance has no relation to the efficacy of ordination.

Our Fathers then, having partly perceived these points, and seeing that the scholastic doctrine concerning the transubstantiation of the bread and wine and the more recent doctrine of the repetition (as was believed) of the sacrifice of the cross in the Mass, were connected by popular feeling with certain of the ceremonies and prayers that followed, asked themselves in what way the whole rite of ordination might not only be brought to greater solidity and purity, but might become more perfect and more noble. And inasmuch as at that time there was nothing known for certain as to the antiquity of the first prayers, but the opinions of learned men assigned all efficacy to the "imperative" forms, they turned their attention to the latter rather than to the former.

With this object therefore in view they first aimed at simplicity, and concentrated the parts of the whole rite as it were on one prominent point, so that no one could doubt at what moment the grace and power of the priesthood was given. For such is the force of simplicity that it lifts men's minds towards divine things more than a long series of ceremonies united by however good a meaning. Therefore having placed in the forefront the prayers which declared both the office of the priesthood and its succession from the ministry of the Apostles, they joined the laying on of hands with our Lord's own words. And in this matter they intentionally followed the example of the Apostolic Church, which first "fell to prayer" and then laid on hands and sent forth its ministers, not that of the Roman Church, which uses laying on of hands before the prayers. . . .

We therefore, taking our stand on Holy Scripture, make reply that in the ordering of Priests we do duly lay down and set forth the stewardship and ministry of the word and Sacraments, the power of remitting and retaining sins, and other functions of the pastoral office, and that in these we do sum up and rehearse all other functions. Indeed the Pope himself is a witness to this, who especially derives the honour of the Pontifical tiara from Christ's triple commendation of His flock to the penitent S. Peter. Why then does he suppose that, which he holds so honourable in his own case, to contribute nothing to the dignity and offices of the priesthood in the case of Anglican Priests?

XX. Finally, we would have our revered brother in Christ beware lest in expressing this judgment he do injustice not only to us but to other Christians also, and among them to his own predecessors, who surely enjoyed in an equal measure with himself the gift of the Holy Spirit.

For he seems to condemn the Orientals, in company with ourselves, on account of defective intention, who in the *"Orthodox Confession"* issued about 1640 name only two functions of a sacramental priesthood, that is to say that of absolving sins and of preaching; who in the *"Longer Russian Catechism"* (Moscow, 1839) teach nothing about the sacrifice of the Body and Blood of Christ, and mention among the offices which pertain to Order only those of ministering the Sacraments and feeding the flock. Further, it thus speaks of the three Orders: "The Deacon serves at the Sacraments; the Priest hallows the Sacraments, in dependence on the Bishop; the Bishop not only hallows the Sacraments himself, but has the power also to impart to others by the laying on of his hands the gift and grace to hallow them." The Eastern Church is assuredly at one with us in teaching that the ministry of more than one mystery describes the character of the priesthood better than the offering of a single sacrifice.

This indeed appears in the form used in the Greek Church to-day in the prayer beginning *O God who art great in power:*—"Fill this man, whom Thou hast chosen to attain the rank of Presbyter, with the gift of Thy Holy Spirit, that he may be worthy blamelessly to assist at Thy Sanctuary, to preach the Gospel of Thy Kingdom, to minister the Word of Thy Truth, to offer Thee spiritual gifts and sacrifices, to renew Thy people by the laver of regeneration," etc.

But let the Romans consider now not once or twice what judgment they will pronounce upon their own Fathers, whose ordinations we have described above. For if the Pope shall by a new decree declare our Fathers of two hundred and fifty years ago wrongly ordained, there is nothing to hinder the inevitable sentence that by the same law all who have been similarly ordained have received no orders. And if our Fathers, who used in 1550 and 1552 forms which as he says are null, were altogether unable to reform them in 1662, his own Fathers come under the self-same law. And if Hippolytus and Victor and Leo and Gelasius and Gregory have some of them said too little in their rites about the priesthood and the high priesthood, and nothing about the power of offering the sacrifice of the Body and Blood of Christ, the Church of Rome herself has an invalid priesthood, and the reformers of the Sacramentaries, no matter what their names, could do nothing to remedy her rites. "For as the Hierarchy (to use the Pope's words) had become extinct on account of the nullity of the form, there remained no power of ordaining." And if the Ordinal "was wholly insufficient to confer Orders, it was impossible that in the course of time it could become sufficient, since no change has taken place. In vain those who from the [VIth and XIth centuries] have attempted to hold some kind of sacrifice or of priesthood, [and power of remitting and retaining sins], have made some additions to the Ordinal." Thus in overthrowing our orders, he overthrows all his own, and pronounces sentence on his own Church. Eugenius IVth indeed brought his Church into great peril of nullity when he taught a new matter and a new form of Order and left the real without a word. For no one knows how many ordinations may have been made, according to his teaching, without any laying on of hands or appropriate form. Pope Leo demands a form unknown to previous Bishops of Rome, and an intention which is defective in the catechisms of the Oriental Church.

To conclude, since all this has been laid before us in the name of peace and unity, we wish it to be known to all men that we are at least equally zealous in our devotion to peace and unity in the Church. We acknowledge that the things which our brother Pope Leo XIIIth has written from time to time in other letters are sometimes very true and always written with a good will. For the difference and debate between us and him arises from a diverse interpretation of the self-same Gospel, which we all believe and honour as the only true one. We also gladly declare that there is much in his own person that is worthy of love and reverence. But that error, which is inveterate in the Roman communion, of substituting the visible head for the invisible Christ, will rob his good words of any fruit of peace. Join with us then, we entreat you, most reverend brethren, in weighing patiently what Christ intended when He established the ministry of His Gospel. When this has been done, more will follow as God wills in His own good time.

God grant that, even from this controversy, may grow fuller knowledge of the truth, greater patience, and a broader desire for peace, in the Church of Christ the Saviour of the world!

F. CANTUAR:
WILLELM: EBOR:

Dated on Friday the 19th day of February A.D. 1897.